GPAC
10/98

DESIGNER
TECHNIQUES

Couture Tips for
Home Sewing

KENNETH D. KING

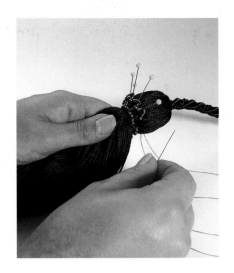

DESIGNER
TECHNIQUES
Couture Tips for Home Sewing

KENNETH D. KING

Sterling Publishing Co., Inc.
New York

A Sterling/Sewing Information Resources Book

Owner: JoAnn Pugh-Gannon
Photography: John Bagley, San Francisco, Ca.
Book Design and Electronic Page Layout: Rose Sheifer, Graphic Productions
Illustrations: Ginny Coull, Coull Art & Design
Index: Anne Leach
Production provided by Jennings and Keefe, Corte Madera, Ca.
Publishing Director: Jack Jennings
Project Manager: Kari Popovic

Every effort has been made to ensure that all the information in this book is accurate.
However, due to differing conditions, tools, and individual skills, the publisher cannot
be responsible for any injuries, losses, and other damages which may result from the
use of the information in this book.

Sewing Information Resources is a registered trademark of GANZ Inc.

A Sterling/Sewing Information Resources Book

Library of Congress Cataloging-in-Publication Data Available.

10 9 8 7 6 5 4 3 2 1

First paperback edition published in 1998 by
Sterling Publishing Company, Inc.
387 Park Avenue South, New York, N.Y. 10016
© 1996 by Kenneth D. King
Distributed in Canada by Sterling Publishing
% Canadian Manda Group, One Atlantic Avenue, Suite 105
Toronto, Ontario, Canada M6K 3E7
Distributed in Great Britain and Europe by Cassell PLC
Wellington House, 125 Strand, London WC2R 0BB, England
Distributed in Australia by Capricorn Link (Australia) Pty Ltd.
P.O. Box 6651, Baulkham Hills, Business Centre, NSW 2153, Australia
Printed in Hong Kong
All rights reserved

Sterling ISBN 0-8069-9489-4 Trade
              0-8069-9490-8 Paper

The following Kenneth D. King designs were graciously offered
for use in photography for this book:

Before Beginning
Midnight blue velvet cape (page 6) from the collection of Tate Cohn.

Designer Edge Finishes
Triple-layer multi-colored organza skirt (page 30) from the collection of
Peggy Welzenbach.

Piping for Apparel and Home
Black wool jacket with piping trim (page 39) from the collection of
Peggy Welzenbach.

Pockets
Black faille dinner jacket and yellow Thai silk vest (page 71) from the
collection of Peggy Welzenbach.

Finishing Touches
Deep violet tasseled handbag with pleated fabric trim (page 100) from
the collection of Peggy Welzenbach.

CONTENTS

INTRODUCTION

Some of my customers ask me, "Why are you writing a book?"Aside from the obvious (because some nice people will give me money for it), it's a chance for me to talk to an audience that speaks the same language of sewing. An audience that, like me, considers sewing a passion. Besides, nobody at the cocktail parties I go to understands my sewing jokes!

For those of you who don't know much about me, I started sewing young, and worked in window display before becoming a designer. Display was useful training, since a good display person has to have a working knowledge of a broad range of subjects. This training taught me to connect information from different disciplines to achieve a desired result.

I have little formal sewing training beyond pattern drafting with a French-trained teacher. All my sewing skills have been self-taught. In certain respects this has proved beneficial, since I was *just* ignorant enough of the facts to do what I wanted. This lack of formal training makes me find some rather unorthodox solutions to construction problems.

I am one of the fortunate few who is able to make my livelihood from the vocation that is also my passion. Since I am deeply interested in what I do, and since I have chosen to sell in a very demanding market, I am called upon to create superbly finished and well-performing products that are also profit-generating. This is most important. I have also been forced to conceive techniques that will give me the proper finish while making good use of my time.

It is some of these unique techniques that I have chosen to share in this book. These techniques have many applications for everyone who sews. With a little practice and some creative thinking, you will be able to make some pieces that will amaze you! And hopefully there will be more books to follow.

In the sewing literature available today, there is an emphasis on shortcuts and other time-saving procedures. Some of them are dandy, but some *look* like you were trying to save time or money! I believe it's better to spend a bit more time with a project and achieve something very special rather than save the time or money sewing running shorts and t-shirts. Let those factories that can do the work more cost-effectively do it. In other words, extra time in today's hectic world is indeed a luxury; when taking time for sewing make that luxury count!

Now for a word on how to use this book. As you will see, this book is not really project-oriented, rather it's a book devoted to techniques. One reason for this is that I regard techniques as tools, or what I refer to as my "bag of tricks." All the information on one subject is grouped together in one section, preceded by new terms (sometimes my own) and their definitions; so if your interest is sewing with velvet, for example, all my tricks with velvet are there. While I hope you will just sit down and read through my book, from cover to cover, not taking nourishment or sleep until you finish because you are so *fascinated* with the information, I know this is not realistic. A very wise woman once told me that it's not necessary to carry around all you need to know in your head, you only have to know where to get your hands on that information when needed. Familiarize yourself with the book (and look at the cool pictures!), and you can then refer to it when you need it.

You will also notice that I refer to the "piece" in the text. These techniques need not be restricted to apparel sewing, they lend themselves to home and craft sewing as well. Keep in mind–*it's all sewing*. The logic and concepts apply, whether it's to clothing, home furnishings, or crafts. My hope is that this book will make traveling across the sewing spectrum a rewarding journey.

There are some sections that could be construed as projects, but the directions given in these function as a point of departure and warn of some of the pitfalls in construction along the way. My wish, though, is for this book to stimulate your sense of creativity and adventure. Don't be afraid to experiment with my techniques. In sewing there are no absolutes. I will be interested in hearing, as I teach and travel, how these techniques directed you to your own creative solutions to sewing challenges.

FABRIC LEGEND

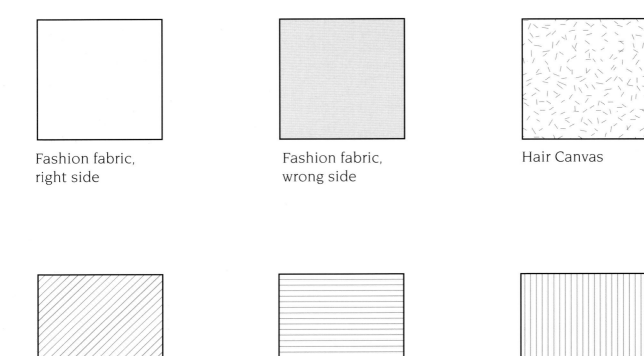

Fashion fabric,
right side

Fashion fabric,
wrong side

Hair Canvas

Horsehair Canvas

Lightweight interwoven

Cheap Fabric

Cheap Fabric,
wrong side

FABRIC LEGEND

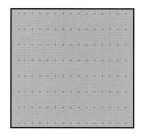

Mohair

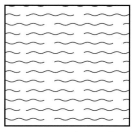

Lining, right side

Lining, wrong side

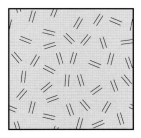

Interlining

Misc. fabric

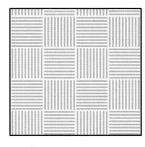

Buckram

Buckram,
diagonal (not a
new pattern)

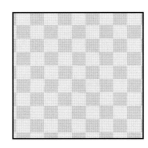

Felt, right side

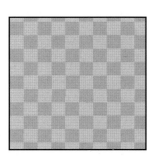

Felt, wrong side

BEFORE BEGINNING

DEFINITIONS

• **Fashion Fabric:** This is the fabric that will be seen in the finished piece. There are no rules regarding what type of fabric to use or whether the right or wrong side should show in the finished piece (sometimes the wrong side of the fabric is more attractive than the right side).

• **Understructure:** A generic term applied to all interfacings, interlinings, and support notions used to create the various effects desired. When your work relies heavily on understructure, it is easy to achieve effects that flatter a figure or even a sofa!

• **Underlining or Interlining:** These terms refer to fabric that is cut the same size as the fashion fabric and then, with both pieces together, treated as one when sewing for support and weight in the finished piece. These terms are often used interchangeably.

• **Interfacing:** The various materials used to stiffen and support the garment, not to be confused with interlining. There is usually a separate pattern piece for the interfacing. Interfacing is either sew-in or fusible and, unless otherwise stated, sew-in interfacing is the type discussed in this book.

• **Lining:** Lining serves two purposes, first, to finish the inside of the piece, and secondly, for aesthetics. It is very satisfying to the sewer to know the inside of the piece is as beautiful as the outside, even when no one else sees the lining.

CHOOSING FASHION FABRICS

The choice of fashion fabric is an entirely personal decision. If the fabric speaks to you, ignore family and friends, and even your own better judgment, and just use it. Here are some words of wisdom on some difficult fabrics.

The fabrics that are most apt to cause problems are velvet, moiré, faille (also known as bengaline), ottoman, and satin. Once you know the pitfalls of working with these fabrics, you will feel more comfortable dealing with them.

WORKING WITH VELVET

Velvet is one of those fabrics that is often referred to as having psychological components. One component is the expectation of weight, the other is the expectation of thickness or a "cushion." When you put your hands on velvet, you expect your fingers to just sink into the fabric.

To achieve this effect when working with velvet, interline all pieces with cotton flannel (see "Understructure"). Interlining with cotton flannel gives the fabric a richer hand. It also allows you to hand-tack the seam allowances using a feather stitch, eliminating any topstitching that might be needed to control seam allowances. The very idea of topstitching velvet gives some folks nightmares! Flannel used for baby's night wear can be used here. It is inexpensive, especially in end-of-bolt pieces on the discount tables, and provides some comic relief to know that inside a couture piece resides a teddy bear print.

After preshrinking the interlining, cut the garment pieces out of both the velvet and flannel. Mark all your seamlines on the flannel piece. Treat the two pieces as one by tailor basting them together with silk thread. The silk thread will prevent needle and thread marks from showing on the velvet.

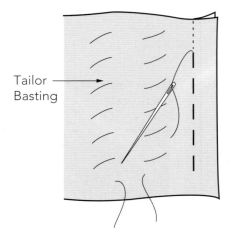

Tailor Basting

When sewing velvet to a flat-surfaced fabric, there is no way around it—baste as if your life depended on it! With velvet-to-velvet seams, pin-basting can be substituted. By marking the seamlines on the flannel, the "creep" in velvet is controlled by hand- or pin-basting the seamlines together and it allows for more accurate sewing.

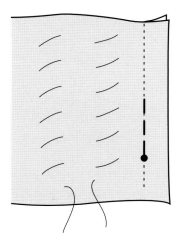

The stitch quality is most important when sewing on velvet, especially on straight seams, which have a tendency to pucker. Since you are working with some thickness, use a stitch length that is longer than normal. A slight zigzag also helps minimize the puckering. Using a walking foot is an absolute necessity for controlling all of the layers. Buy one—you will bless the day you did.

Machine Settings—Sewing Machine
Stitch: Zigzag
Stitch Width: 0.5 mm
Stitch Length: 3.0–3.5 mm

TIP
On velvet, the zigzag stitch is especially effective when the seam falls on the bias, as in a gored skirt. The stitch is long enough to minimize the puckering, and the zigzag builds in additional stretch.

Once you have sewn the seams, now comes the arduous task of pressing. Most stitchers prefer pressing velvet using either a heavy towel or a velvet pressing board. But many people end up crushing the nap of the fabric at the edge of the board, since most velvet pressing boards are on the small side.

From my design experience, I have found that the best surface for pressing velvet is *mohair* velvet. Remember that prickly velvet sofa your grandmother had? That fabric is mohair velvet, and it's still being made today for upholstery. Purchase a piece large enough to cover the entire surface of your pressing table. Having this large a pressing surface is particularly helpful when pressing pieces with long seams, such as a full-length skirt. There is no edge on which to mar the nap and there is no need to move the pressing board to press a long seam. When you compare them by size, a piece of mohair velvet is far less expensive than a velvet board.

Before pressing, trim the seam allowances of the flannel to ¼". To press, lay the piece flat, right side down, on the mohair velvet. Steam and finger-press the seams open. If you are using an industrial steam iron, keep the iron well away from the fabric—the heavy jets of steam will crush the nap. Test the steam on an

TIP
When stitching velvet collars and cuffs, pad the velvet with a thin layer of cotton or wool batting (don't use polyester, whatever they say, as it may "bleed" through the velvet). This extra padding technique is also effective for hats, handbags or wherever a feeling of luxury is desired.

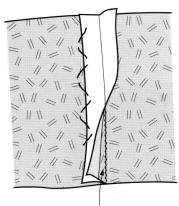

Flannel trimmed to ¼"

extra piece of fabric first.

Once the seams are pressed, use a feather stitch to attach the seam allowances to the flannel.

Besides thickness another expectation with velvet is weight. The flannel interlining does add some weight, but additional weight can be added by interfacing the hem with bias strips of wool melton making a soft fold at the hem.

Or interface the hem with horsehair braid and add weights along the hem. This technique works especially well with gored skirts or swing-back coats. Attach the weights where the seamlines meet the hem.

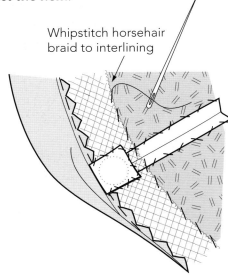

Whipstitch horsehair braid to interlining

This controls the drape quite nicely and allows graceful movement when the piece is in motion. Be careful though, too much weight makes the piece oppressive to wear.

To cover weights, cut a piece of fabric or felt twice the diameter of the weight plus ½" all around for seam allowances. Fold the fabric in half. Using an adjustable zipper foot, stitch the weight into the fold of the fabric running the foot along the edge of the weight. Grade the seam allowances and hand-stitch the covered weight into the piece.

FAILLE (OR BENGALINE), MOIRÉ, AND OTTOMAN

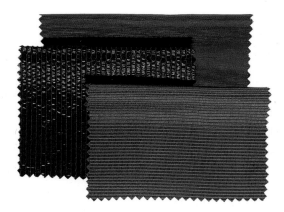

These fabrics are often referred to as "corded" fabrics, because the warp threads are fairly fine, while the weft threads are of a heavy cotton. In faille and moiré, the crosswise threads are fine and packed closely together, but with ottoman the large cords are spaced further apart. This method of construction creates a ribbed effect along the crosswise grain.

These fabrics may shrink under steam. The degree of shrinkage is dependent on how thick the crosswise threads are and whether or not there was pressure used in the finishing process. In the moiré process, the optical effect of the moiré is pressed onto the ribbed surface of the fabric with heat. Therefore, preshrink with steam before cutting into ottomans and failles. And on moirés, avoid preshrinking like the plague! Since the crosswise threads are cotton (a natural fiber), the moiré effect will not last under steam—the fibers will plump up and the moiré effect will be diminished or lost.

When pressing these fabrics, also be careful not to create impressions of the fabric against itself. Use a pressing surface covered with cotton drill cloth or any other smooth covering to avoid creating additional undesired textures on the fabrics.

These fabrics can easily be used for vests and tailored clothing, as well as home furnishings. Since they are somewhat perishable, always use an interlining of some sort. For clothing, siri cotton or cotton flannel works quite nicely. In home furnishings, cotton flannel or wool flannel will give a good result.

> ### TIP
>
> When making something white or an extremely light color in a rayon moiré or bengaline, Scotchgard™ the fabric to death to help keep it fresh. With these fabrics, if there was a bad crease in the fabric that has been pressed out, Scotchgard™ will make it reappear, never to leave. Better safe than sorry! Always test first.

SATIN

Use a heavy slipper satin for most purposes, either for apparel or home furnishings. Satin makes dandy linings and works up well in a piece giving it nice body.

When marking, use a marking wheel with either a smooth edge or one with blunted points. The sharper pointed wheels will tear the fabric. Use silk thread and a #10 beading needle when making tailor's tacks on satin. The beading needle and silk thread should be used for any thread tracing or basting that is needed.

It is necessary to interline satin if it is to be used for tailored garments or any outer garment. For home furnishings, it is also a good idea to interline. For apparel, interline with cotton flannel. For home projects, cotton or a cotton/poly blend twill is best, as these fabrics will take the strain of daily use.

When pressing satin, use a dry iron. Steam just makes the surface of satin "wobbly" and is used only in those cases where a soft press is desired. When hard-pressing a seam open, first press the seam as sewn, then press it open on a hard wooden seam roll that is covered with cotton drill cloth (see section on "Equipment and Tools").

On certain satin pieces, such as the luxurious lining of an evening wrap, a soft press of the seams is desirable. After pressing as sewn, lay the seam over the seam roll, and steam lightly for a cushioned effect. Finger-press the seam open forming a softly creased seamline.

UNDERSTRUCTURE MATERIALS AND NOTIONS

Remember this saying: "The fashion fabric is only along for the ride!"

The understructure materials discussed here are those that will be referred to throughout this book. As you will discover, some of the materials you will use in your future projects may be unorthodox and are often not used as the manufacturer intended. All interfacings referred to are sew-in interfacings, unless otherwise noted. Unless indicated, preshrinking is necessary for all understructures. The preferred method is to take wool fabrics to the dry cleaners and have them heavily steamed. Cotton fabrics can be washed and dried at home.

Wool Felt adds heft and thickness to a piece and should be as high a percentage of wool as possible. Use it for interlining small pieces, or spot interlining on large ones, as well as interfacing hems for a better drape.

> ### TIP
>
> Wool felt is increasingly difficult to find, since most of the world's felt is produced in the unstable eastern bloc countries. If you can get it, buy the entire bolt!

Wool Flannel can be used if wool felt is not available. It also gives heft to home decorating fabrics, as well as clothing projects. Wool flannel is warm, so if the piece needs just a nice heft or weight use cotton flannel. Interline evening wraps or coats with wool flannel. When washed in hot water and dried at a high temperature, you will create your own wool felt.

Wool Melton is a coat fabric that is very useful for interfacing hems of jackets or thickening collars. It's also a good substitute (although a relatively expensive one) for wool felt. If a flat sleeve head is desired for tailoring, wool melton is a good choice. Buy end-of-bolt pieces from the remnant tables, as buying it from the regular-priced bolt can be expensive.

Hair Canvas is used for interfacing tailored clothes. Hymo is the best choice because of its drape and weight. It's made from a blend of wool and goat hair which causes the hymo to "stick" to the fashion fabric. Avoid fusible hair canvas for most applications when using the methods outlined in this book.

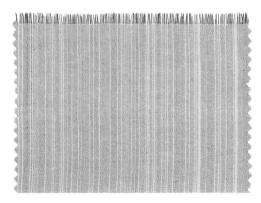

Horsehair Canvas or **Haircloth** is available in two varieties. Traditionally made from real horsehair, there is another type made from nylon. The real horsehair is the way to go if you can find it. It's about 18"–20" wide (the length of the horse's tail), with the hair running in the crosswise grain. The nylon horsehair can be wider.

The characteristic of this fabric that is so useful in construction is the difference between the stability on the crosswise grain versus the fluidity of the lengthwise grain. In jackets, use horsehair canvas for shields, as well as flat shoulder pads.

You can also use haircloth for cut-and-sewn hats. Stiffening with haircloth is better for this type of hat because it springs back into shape when crushed. Buckram loses its starch after awhile.

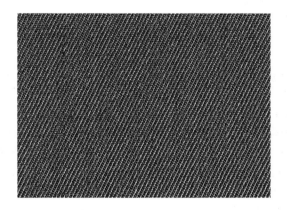

Twill Fabric is used as interlining in pieces that will receive stress through stretch such as home decorating projects. Run the grainline parallel to the line of stretch to absorb the stress on the fashion fabric. All of the stretch needs to be gone from the fabric, so do not preshrink.

Cotton Flannel is a favorite for interlinings. You can often find bolt ends of children's pajama fabric for your projects. It will cause you no end of delight knowing some of the pieces you have are interlined with teddy bears or toy trucks.

Drapery Interlining Flannel is quite sumptuous and hangs well. This fabric works well with silks, lightweight jacquards, moirés, and failles.

Siri Cotton is used when an interlining is needed but insulation is not an issue. Siri cotton is appropriate for slightly heavier fabrics, such as moiré, faille, or bengaline, where hemming and tacking down facings would show through.

Armo© Press Soft is used interchangeably with siri cotton. You may find that this product is often pulled off-grain when it is wound onto the bolt. Check the grainline and straighten it before cutting.

Cotton Batiste works nicely under wool crepe, when a slight bit of control is desired to help the garment keep its shape. Batiste also works well for making the half-back interfacing pieces for tailored jackets.

Organza can either be polyester or silk. The polyester has more bounce and may or may not be to your taste when pressing. Organza works well when interlining or facing bodices of bias-cut or other slinky dresses, where light-weight interlining and a slight bit of control at the bust is desired. It also makes terrific stay tape, and is good for interfacing welt pockets when bulk is not desired.

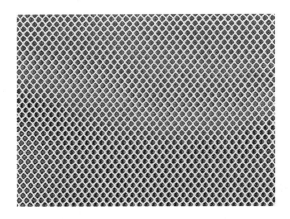

Heavy Net or Nylon Buckram is useful for stiffening laces, creating petticoats, or making supports for those "man-eating" puffed sleeves. To give you an idea of how stiff this net is, compare nylon net to silk tulle. Heavy net is to nylon net what nylon net is to silk tulle. It is the chain link fence of net.

Batting provides a padding making velvets or furs feel more luxurious. Select silk, cotton, or wool battings, as the polyesters tend to shed over time.

Twill Tape is one product used for stabilizing seams and roll lines, as well as pocket edges. It is generally better to use twill tape with heavier fabrics, using organza for lightweight fabrics.

Rattail Cord is a decorative satin cord that comes in two widths—¹⁄₁₆" and ⅛". Beside the decorative uses, you can use rattail cord for the fill in piping (see "Piping"). It is rigid and smooth giving an even thickness to finished piped edges. When purchased by the bolt, it is quite inexpensive.

TREATMENT OF INTERFACINGS NOT STITCHED INTO SEAMS

The method outlined here is an alternative to using fusible interfacings, one which you can use in tailoring, as well as at other times when stiffening a seam is not desirable. This method also eliminates any mishaps from fusibles "bubbling," or otherwise looking strange, after coming back from the abusive dry cleaner.

1. When cutting the interfacing piece, use a nonfusible hair canvas, or any other desired interfacing. Cut out the interfacing pieces from the canvas, and also out of a "thin cheap" fabric. Place the two layers together with the "thin cheap" fabric on the wrong side of the canvas next to the fashion fabric. Pin together.

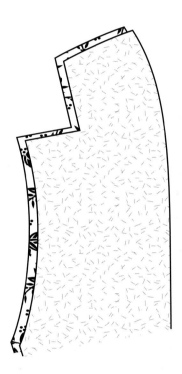

2. Place the cut edge on the 1" mark on the throat plate and zigzag the pieces together. The serpentine stitch is a very strong alternative stitch. By placing the "thin cheap" fabric on the wrong side of the canvas next to the fashion fabric, the cut edge of the interfacing won't leave an impression on the fabric when pressing later. The seam allowances of the interfacing are trimmed close to the stitching.

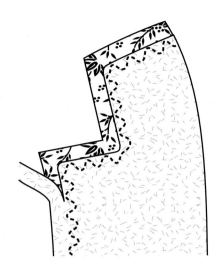

3. The excess "thin cheap" fabric is cut away from the body of the piece.

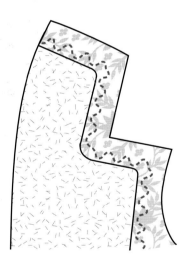

4. Baste the fashion fabric to the interfacing/"thin cheap" fabric unit with silk thread. Basting may seem to take more time than it's worth, but the result is far better.

TREATMENT FOR HORSEHAIR CANVAS ON THE BIAS

When using horsehair canvas on the bias, such as in hat or jacket construction when a bias cut ensures a snug and comfortable fit, ripples will often occur. This becomes a problem, especially when the fashion fabric has a smooth finish like satin or gabardine. Follow the method outlined here to put tension on the horsehair canvas and smooth out the ripples.

1. Following the procedure outlined for "Treatment of Interfacings not Stitched into Seams," prepare the horsehair canvas/"thin cheap" fabric unit.

2. Using fusible web, fuse together a piece of wool felt and a piece of hair canvas large enough to accommodate the pattern piece. Fuse the hair canvas to the felt before cutting out the pattern piece, as the canvas will shrink when fused. Match the grainlines of the horsehair/"thin cheap" fabric unit with the grainlines of the felt/canvas unit. Cut out the pattern piece from the fused felt unit, keeping in mind that the felt side will be next to the fashion fabric, so lay out the pattern pieces accordingly.

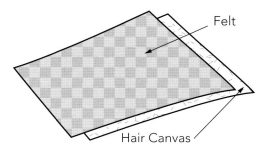

Felt

Hair Canvas

3. Lay the felt/canvas unit on top of the horsehair unit and pin in place.

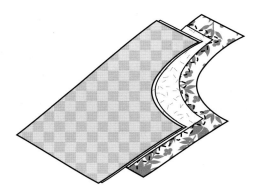

4. Zigzag all layers together, stitching rows about ½" apart. The zigzag will bond the two layers together while retaining the stretch of the bias. Keep the rows of stitching inside the cut edge of the horsehair unit.

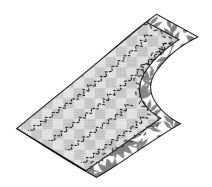

5. Place the fashion fabric piece on top of the entire interfacing unit, right sides up. Baste all layers together within the seam allowance. You are now ready to continue construction of your garment or piece.

EQUIPMENT AND TOOLS

It goes without saying that a good sewing machine and a serger are really needed in today's sewing room. There are also many new presser feet on the market to make quick work of most sewing projects.

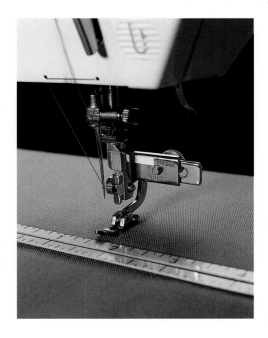

Adjustable Zipper Foot: The one used here is ¼" wide, adjustable, and can be attached to any machine, either with the presser foot set screw attached directly to the shaft, or with an adapter. It is essential that a ¼"-wide foot be used with the "Piped Pockets and Buttonholes" techniques outlined in the chapter "Piping for Apparel and the Home," but a slightly wider foot can be used with the other methods.

You will come to prefer the adjustable foot for two reasons, control and flexibility. With the adjustable foot, you can control exactly where the needle is positioned in relation to the foot. When using the zipper foot included with your machine, sometimes the needle positions are not out far enough for the purposes of the techniques outlined here. With the adjustable foot you can see exactly where the needle is and therefore have better control of your stitching.

This foot is not used just for applying zippers. The welt pocket is sewn more easily with the adjustable zipper foot than with the regular presser foot. You will also appreciate this foot for piped corners and lined patch pockets.

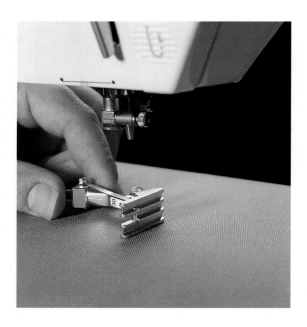

3-Groove Pintuck Foot: Besides making a dandy pintuck when used with the double needle, the 3-groove pintuck foot can be used to make the "Rolled Hem on Sheer Fabrics" and "French Seams with the Sewing Machine and Serger" discussed in the next chapter. Available from the same manufacturer as your sewing machine, or purchased as a generic foot, with some practice this foot can also be used to install invisible zippers.

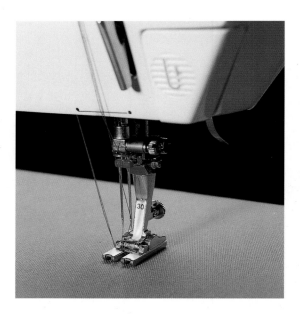

Double Needles: Double needles are available in a variety of sizes and are labeled with two numbers. The first number is the distance between the needles. This distance must correspond to the width of the central channel in the pintuck foot. The second number is the size of the needles themselves. Experiment with the different needle sizes available to choose the right needles for your purpose.

Irons: Next to a good sewing machine and a serger, the most important piece of equipment in your sewing room is a really good iron. There are a number of very good household irons on the market, but if you really want to go to town with pressing, get an industrial iron that has a gravity feed water supply. Gravity has no moving parts! The volume of steam on demand is really what this type of iron is all about.

Besides gravity feed, another thing to look for in an iron is weight. Purchase the heaviest iron you can manage, as a heavier iron holds heat longer because of its composition. Though easier to hold and lift, the heat retention on the lighter-weight irons is just not there. Nothing is more frustrating than having to wait for the iron to heat back up for more steam.

Steamer: A "jiffy" steamer is a really dandy tool that is normally seen in clothing stores and is used to steam out garments. Great when shaping with steam, the nozzle is flexible and lighter in weight than an iron. A steamer comes in handy, especially when doing millinery or other work where a constant stream of gentle steam is desired. This gentle and constant steam is better for velvet, since the steam coming from the ports of the industrial iron can sometimes flatten the nap.

For a budget substitute, go to a thrift store and purchase an inexpensive tea kettle. Buy a length of dishwasher hose at the hardware store and tape one end of the hose to the spout of the kettle. Fill the tea kettle with water and put it on to boil. Wrap a hot pad around the other end of the hose to protect your hands and, voila, a steamer! Once you're finished with your steaming, you can have tea, too!

Puff Iron: Also known as a pressing egg, this device looks like a steel egg on a post. It clamps to your pressing table and has a high/low temperature switch. If you wish to regulate the temperature more precisely, there are devices on the market to do this. These regulators can be found in craft catalogues that sell soldering irons or wood burning tools. Puffed sleeves, millinery, smocking, and ruffle pressing are quick work with the puffing iron.

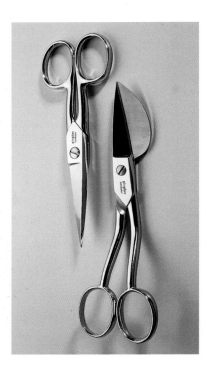

Scissors: Along with the usual complement of shears for cutting fabric, the tailor's point scissors and appliqué scissors are good to have on hand. Tailor's point scissors are about 4"–5" long and have thick spines along the back of the blades. They cut easily through many layers of fabric and can clip right up to a point since the tips of the blades will not separate. Appliqué scissors have what looks like a pelican bill on one blade. This flat blade pushes aside the fabric that is not cut when trimming appliqués. This action is also helpful when grading seams. Another good feature to look

for when shopping for scissors is the combination of a forward fulcrum and thick spines along the backs of the blades. This combination gives strength, power, and control when cutting.

Pressing Table: Have this table built for your studio and you will find that you cannot live without it. The pressing surface is 24"x 60" and the table is 38" high. Pad the top with cotton batting and cover it using a canvas cover with a 1" grid printed on it.

> **TIP**
>
> Whenever possible, pressing surfaces should be wood covered with cotton. This surface draws the steam and heat through the piece for more effective pressing. Teflon covers on the market produce an inferior result, as they reflect heat back.

The large pressing surface enables you to press a full 60"-wide fabric easily. Underneath you can build a shelf for pressing tools, and attach cup hooks on the side to hang seam rolls, brushes, and so on. On the side of the pressing table, mount a plug strip with an on-off switch. You can plug your iron and the light over the table into the plug strip. The little red light on irons is sometimes too subtle to see. If you see the light on over the table, you know the iron is still on!

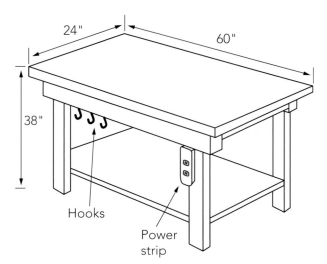

Hooks

Power strip

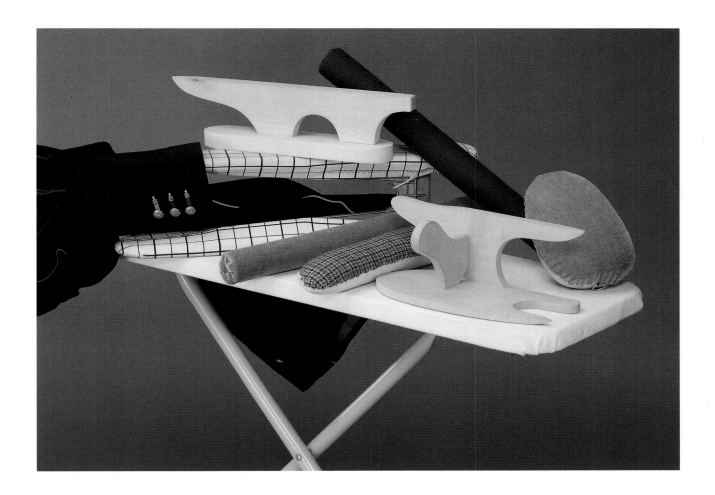

Seam Rolls: Make your own seam rolls, as the ones sold commercially are too soft for my taste. Pressing with a hard seam roll gives a flatter seam that will almost disappear. Closet rod dowels are best, although half-round hardwood molding works nicely, too. Cover one in cotton drill for smooth fabrics, cover another in wool flannel for wools, and cover a third in mohair velvet for velvets and other napped fabrics. Hang them from the side of your pressing table to store.

Sleeve and Other Pressing Boards: A sleeve board is very helpful for pressing many difficult areas. They are available from a tailor's supply or in the notions department of fabric stores. Have a variety of smaller pressing boards that can sit on the pressing table giving you more flexibility in pressing different sized pieces. They are all wood, lightly padded, and are covered with cotton drill.

Pressing Ham: Purchase the regulation model, but cover one side in mohair velvet.

The "Horse": This device is used to drape fabric over after pressing. Make the top from a sono tube, 12" in diameter and about 4' long. Cover with a matte-finished fabric to keep the pressed fabric set on it from slipping. The tube is supported on two uprights that measure at least 4' long and are connected to wheels. The curve of the tube prevents creasing of the pressed articles and the wheels allow easy transportation.

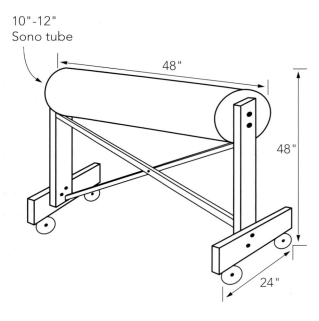

10"-12"
Sono tube

48"

48"

24"

MARKING TOOLS

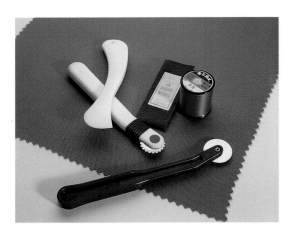

Besides the tracing wheels and carbon papers that are normally in the sewing studio, here are some favorites that perform consistently.

Disappearing Chalk: Clo-chalk or slo-chalk can be purchased from a tailor's supply or through a sewing notions company. This product disappears in 90 hours or with a bit of steam. Since this chalk is air/water soluble, remember that the higher the humidity the faster it disappears. Work fast on rainy days! It can be used on silk without leaving an oil spot, and will leave no residue on satins or taffetas. The only disadvantage is, like clay chalk, it needs to be sharpened to create a crisp line and will break when dropped. However, if dropped and broken, the pieces can be pounded up into powder and put into a chalk wheel. This solves both problems at once.

Pounce Pad: This tool comes from the sign painting world, and a variation is also used at the House of Lesage in Paris for marking embroidery. This high-tech pad is about $10.00 at sign shops,

and you may wish to have two, one for light-colored powder and one for dark. If you prefer a low-tech tool, put cornstarch into a clean white tennis sock and knot the end. When not in use store the sock in a plastic bag.

To use a pounce pad, pierce holes in your paper pattern where chalk marks are desired, using a needle wheel or stitch on your unthreaded sewing machine. After the paper pattern is laid onto the fabric, rub the pounce pad over it to mark. The powder sifts through the holes in the paper, marking the fabric. At Lesage, dark powder is "fixed" to the fabric by spraying with denatured alcohol.

Dual Tracing Wheel: Many European patterns are drafted without seam allowances. The dual tracing wheel, along with carbon paper, is used to add seam allowances to the fabric. It is more accurate, as there is now a seamline marked onto the fabric. Sometimes, seams are stretched or eased before sewing and so the width of the seam allowance is changed. If the piece was just sewn with the standard $\frac{5}{8}$" mark on the machine, the seamline would not be accurate. Though you may think it a silly waste of time, after using this tool for awhile you'll find it gives a more accurate result to all your sewing.

Hera Marker: A tracing wheel can distort or damage the surface of some fabrics. When working with sheer or delicate fabrics, substitute a hera marker, which functions like a thumbnail making an indentation or crease in the fabric. Used alone or with carbon paper, it's also good for creasing paper or taffeta when heat is not desired.

DESIGNER EDGE FINISHES

DEFINITIONS

- **Chain:** Produced by the serger when overlocking a seam. The chain will form the base of the rolled hem outlined in this chapter.
- **Favoring:** A specified amount of fabric is cut from one edge of the seam allowance and a corresponding amount is added to the other. When stitched and pressed, the seam will roll toward the underside. Use this technique on facings or lapels so the edge seam will fall to the back side and be invisible.

- **Machine Easing:** Shorten the stitch length and while the fabric is passing under the foot press your index finger down behind the presser foot. This causes the fabric to ease in front of your finger.

Working with sheer fabrics may be something you get dragged screaming and kicking to, as there is no place to hide. Finishing a hem on sheer fabrics such as chiffon or organza is traditionally done by hand-rolling. However, hand-rolling can be uneven unless you have had a lot of practice. This section should be subtitled "How you can avoid hand-rolling chiffon and feel really clever at the same time." The techniques outlined in this chapter work equally well on chiffon, organza, or other lightweight fabrics.

ROLLED HEM ON SHEER FABRICS

To complete this technique, you will use your sewing machine, your serger, and a 3-groove pintuck foot. Set up your serger for the 3-thread rolled hem.

1. Serge the edge using the 3-thread rolled hem.
Note: If a curved edge is being finished, machine ease first to control the bias. Then, serge over the ease stitching, making sure not to cut off the stitching while serging.

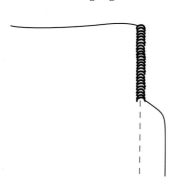

Machine Settings—Serger
Cutting Width: 1
Stitch Length: 1.0–1.5 mm
Differential: 0.7 mm

The fluidity or rigidity of the hem can be regulated by the serger stitch length. The basic rule of thumb is the longer the stitch length, the more fluid the hem.

2. Press the rolled edge toward the body of the piece. Press the edge again, so the entire chain is now rolled under the fabric.

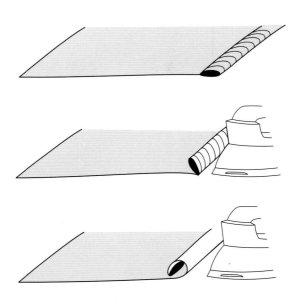

3. Attach a 3-groove pintuck foot to the sewing machine. Move the needle position to a half-left position, and set the machine as follows:

Machine Settings—Sewing Machine
Stitch: Zigzag
Stitch Width: 0.6–0.9 mm
Stitch Length: 0.9–1.2 mm
Thread: Rayon embroidery thread, or monofilament (for metallic fabrics)

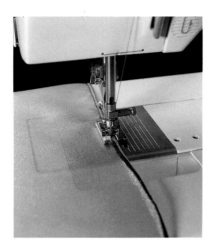

Place the pressed rolled edge, facing up, in the center groove of the pintuck foot, with the body of the piece to the left. Catch the fold of the fabric with the right-hand swing of the needle while sewing. The narrow width setting for the zigzag stitch allows the stitching line to blend with the fold, producing an almost identical appearance on both sides of the rolled hem.

TIP

To get the tightest roll, pull the fabric slightly to the left as it passes under the foot. This will snug the fabric around the serger chain while it is being stitched into place.

FRENCH SEAM WITH THE SEWING MACHINE AND SERGER

Now doesn't that title sound like a contemporary music composition? Once you have mastered the rolled hem, the French seam will be easily understood.

This seam is narrow and strong enough to be used for armhole seams, as long as the seams are not too deeply curved. The finished seam looks like a pintuck, so it can be sewn on the outside of the garment and used as a design element.

You will need to use the favoring technique for this seam. With this method, there is a net loss of $\frac{1}{4}$" on one side of the seam, so you need

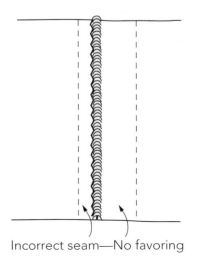

Incorrect seam—No favoring

to compensate by adding ¼" to the other side. In the finished piece, the seam will fall where intended, based on the design.

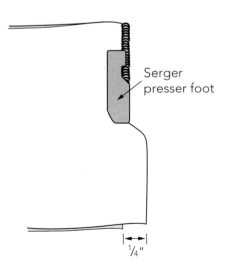

Correct seam—Favored seam

1. Wrong sides together, favor the upper layer of fabric by ¼", as in a classic French seam, and pin.

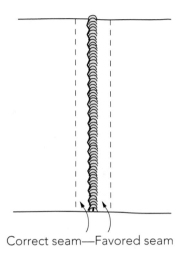

Serger presser foot

¼"

2. If the seamlines fall on the bias (as with gored skirts or gored capes), stay-stitch at ⅜", while slightly machine easing. This keeps the

bias from stretching and dragging the lines of the garment down.

3. Sew a 3-thread rolled hem, placing the cut edge of the upper (favored) layer on the ⅝" mark on the serger.

Machine Settings—Serger
Cutting Width: 1
Differential: 0.7 mm
Stitch Length: 1.2–1.5 mm

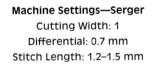

4. Open the seam and press the chain of the rolled hem toward the under layer.

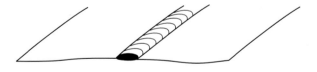

5. Fold the fabric over the rolled hem chain with right sides of the fabric together. By folding the fabric in this manner, the favoring is needed. Otherwise, if favoring wasn't done, the seam would sit to one side of where it is intended in the design.

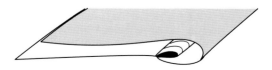

6. Flip the piece over and with the 3-groove pintuck foot on the sewing machine, set the machine needle position to half-left.

Machine Settings—Sewing Machine
Stitch: Zigzag
Stitch Width: 0.6–0.9 mm
Stitch Length: 0.9–1.2 mm
Thread: Rayon embroidery thread, or monofilament (for metallic fabrics)

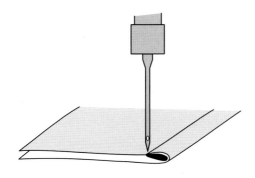

As with the rolled hem, the zigzag stitch falls over the fold making both sides of this seam appear the same. The finished effect is like a pintuck not a seam.

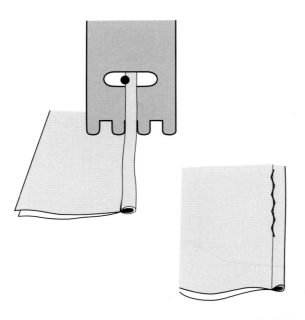

FRENCH SEAM WITH PINTUCK FOOT

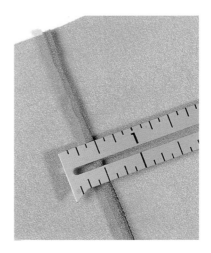

If you don't own a serger, you can achieve a strong, narrow French seam on sheer fabrics using a 3-groove pintuck foot and the appropriately sized double needle. A 3.0/90 needle will be used here.

Refer to the owner's manual for your sewing machine for the correct threading procedure when using double needles. Also, check to be sure that your throat plate can accommodate double needles.

1. With wrong sides together, favor the upper layer of fabric by ¼" and pin.

> ### TIP
> For this procedure, it is preferable to experiment with increasing the upper tension to achieve a ridge when stitching the pintuck. Altering the lower tension will make more work later, since you'll have to readjust the tension back to normal for regular sewing.

2. With the cut edge of the favored layer placed on the ⅝" mark on the throat plate, sew a pintuck. Increase the upper tension causing the pintuck to form a ridge.

3. With a very sharp rotary cutter or appliqué scissors, trim away the excess seam allowance, being careful not to cut through the stitches of the pintuck.

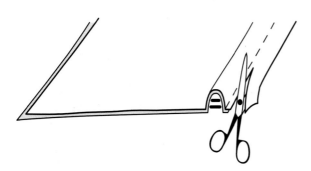

4. Open out the fabric and press lightly so the double row of stitching is facing up.

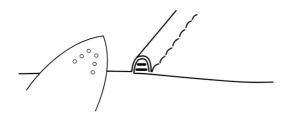

5. Fold right sides together and pin, wrapping the fabric around the pintuck.

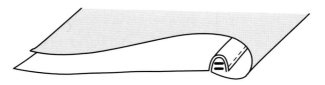

6. Remove the thread from the right needle and return the upper tension to normal. Place the fabric, right side up, under the foot, with the pintuck in the center groove of the foot. The position will be similar to the serger French seam, with the left needle over the fold in the fabric.

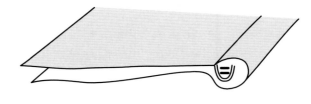

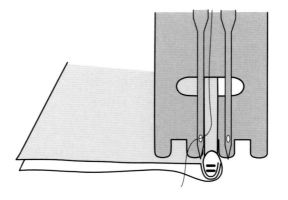

7. Sew with the thread in the left needle. This will produce a straight stitch that closes the seam quite nicely. A slight zigzag can also be used if desired.

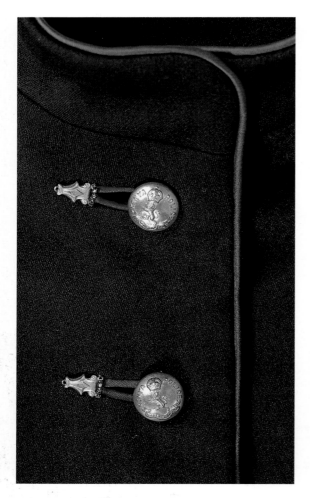

PIPING FOR APPAREL AND THE HOME

DEFINITIONS

• **Bias Cover:** The bias strip of fabric that wraps the fill for piping.

• **Fill:** The element used to stuff piping. Fills are available in many types, from rattail cord to yarn, and in a variety of sizes.

• **Rattail Cord:** Satin cord, about $\frac{1}{8}$" thick, usually used for decorative work but often used as fill. This cord is made of rayon and comes in a variety of colors. For the piping techniques in this book, rattail cord will be used unless otherwise stated.

• **Thinning:** Trimming the fill out of the bias cover when the end of the piping is stitched into a seam. This reduces bulk at the ends of piping.

• **Pocket Bag:** The section of the pocket that holds the contents.

• **Flange:** Refers either to a strip of twill tape functioning like the seam allowance on piping that is stitched to a decorative cord allowing it to be sewn into a seam; or a projection of fabric from a seam used for decorative purposes.

When I met the Curator of Costume at the Los Angeles County Museum of Art, he commented on how much he liked my work and use of piping tricks. To him, "piping is next to Godliness." How true!

For those of you who avoid using piping because you don't like seeing the initial line of stitching that made the piping once the seam is finished, this method is for you!

BASIC PIPED SEAMS

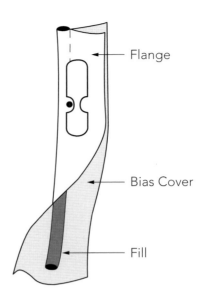

Flange

Bias Cover

Fill

As a general rule, stitch the piping to the fashion fabric for better stability before completing the seams. You will use the ¼" adjustable zipper foot for this technique.

1.   Cut bias strips of fabric 1"–1¼" wide. Stitch bias strips together to make a long continuous strip.

2.   To make piping, adjust the zipper foot so that the needle is as close to the inside of the foot as possible (Position #1). Position #1 is used when making piping and when stitching the piping to a garment after basting but before the other side is sewn in place. Remember, Position #1 is used on anything that is not a final seam.

3.   Wrap the bias strip around the rattail cord and sew using a stitch length of at least 3 mm. Shorter stitches will stiffen and draw up the seam.

4.   To insert piping in a seam, lay a seam gauge down on the piping and push the edge close against the fill. The seam gauge position will be closer to the fill than the first row of stitches. This is as it should be, as the final row of machine stitches will be closer to the fill on the seamline. Then baste the piping in place on the seamline (and we all baste, do we not?). Stitch with the zipper foot in Position #1.

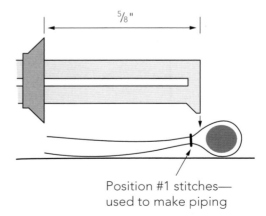

⁵⁄₈"

Position #1 stitches—
used to make piping

5.   To finish the seam, pin right sides together and adjust the zipper foot so the needle is slightly outside the edge of the foot. This

adjustment is Position #2. Remember, Position #2 is for final seams only.

Sew the final seam with the foot in Position #2. In this position, the needle is closer to the rattail fill, causing the previous lines of stitching to fall into the seam allowances. Use a 3 mm or longer stitch to prevent drawing up of the seam.

INSIDE AND OUTSIDE PIPED CORNERS

Straight seams are easy, but the piped corners cause problems for most folks. Here are some tricks you will find helpful when piping inside and outside corners.

Outside corners are most common on vest points or collars and are the easier of the two techniques.

1. When basting the piping to the seamline (yes, basting!), baste to the corner and then measure from the other direction to determine where to pivot. Mark the piping with a marking pen at the pivot point. Make a hand tack with needle and thread on the right side of this mark to secure the piping in place.

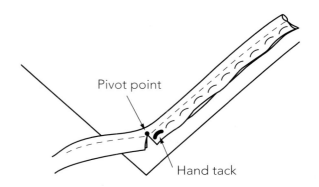

2. Clip the piping seam allowance at the mark and pivot. Push the piping back to the right. The piping will roll back on itself and this is exactly what you want. If this doesn't happen, the corner will round out instead of being square.

3. Make a hand tack with needle and thread on the left side of the pivot mark, and continue basting.

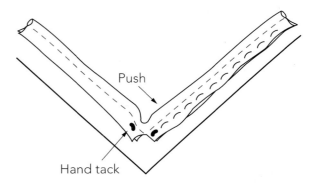

4. To stitch the piping down, place the zipper foot in Position #1 and sew, stopping about ½" before the pivot mark. Shorten the stitch length to 0.3–0.5 mm and continue stitching to the pivot mark. The piping will have to be rolled out of the path of the needle while stitching. Pivot the fabric slightly and stitch one or two stitches across the corner, pivot again, and stitch for another ½". Lengthen the stitch back to normal and continue stitching the piping in place.

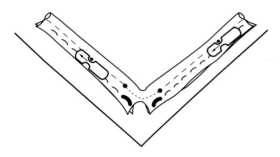

If the corner is fairly sharp, to make turning easier later, stitch a loop of buttonhole twist to the corner of the piping, after the machine stitching is done. Keep this thread from being stitched into the seamline.

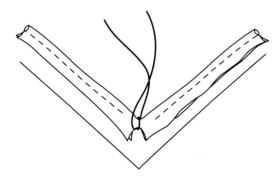

5. To finish the seam, pin right sides together, and baste. Baste the corner using tiny stitches while pinching the fabric together at the machine stitching line and rolling the piping so the machine stitching line is in contact with the fabric on the other side. This is done by feel. Baste along the stitching line to the

pivot point and make a tack stitch. Push the piping back into the piece on the other side (remember, we let the piping roll onto itself in step 2; it now wants to push out of the side not basted) and baste, making sure the machine stitching line is in contact with the fabric on the other side. Finish basting.

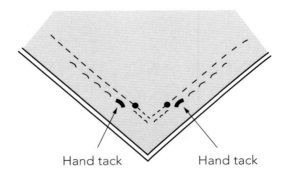

Hand tack   Hand tack

6. Sew the seam with the zipper foot in Position #2, as this is a final seam. Shorten the stitches about ½" away from the corner, making sure the foot is securely against the piping (the rattail is firm enough and will give a good guide). The stitching line will be a scant ¹⁄₁₆" inside the original machine stitching line. Stitch across the corner and up the other side as described before in step 4.

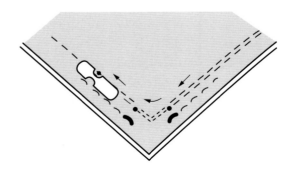

7. Clip the corner, grade the seams, and prepare for turning the corner to the right side. Turn, pulling the loop of buttonhole twist, if used, to turn the corner crisply. Remove the buttonhole twist loop from the seam before pressing.

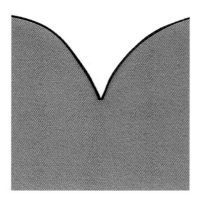

Inside corners are a logical place to end piping, while creating a very nice detail. It looks especially good at the back of a neckline.

1. Beginning at the inside corner, measure to determine where the seam will start. Baste the piping 1" from this point, and trim the seam allowances to ⅛" approximately 2" down the piping.

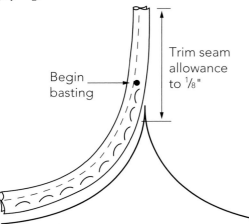

Begin basting

Trim seam allowance to ⅛"

Baste the piping in place all around, ending up at the opposite side of the corner. Trim the seam allowances at this end in the same manner, and baste so that the stitching lines at the ends are ¼" away from one another, adjusting as necessary to keep them centered.

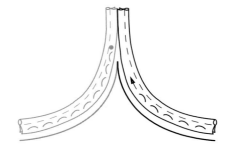

2. Start stitching with the zipper foot in Position #1 and a stitch length of 0.3–0.5 mm. Sew for ½", then lengthen the stitches to 3 mm to attach the piping all along the seam. Then, ½" before the end, shorten the stitches again to finish.

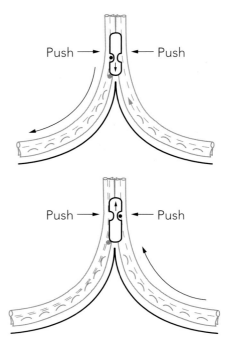

Push → ← Push

Push → ← Push

TIP

Short stitches are used at the corners and the beginning and end of inside corners for two reasons. First, they reinforce the seam for the clipping needed later. Second, they keep the seam from drawing up, as a backstitch would, while still allowing the stitches to be removed one at a time to ensure the corner comes out evenly.

3. With right sides together, pin the two pieces together and put the zipper foot in Position #2. Start stitching with the short stitches for ½", then lengthen to 3 mm to attach the rest of the piece. Shorten the stitches again at the other end, ½" before the stopping point.

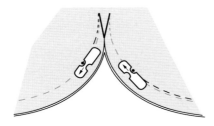

4. Thin the piping ends so the fill will not be caught in the seam. Place a pin through the piping to keep the fill from pulling completely out. Measure from the end of the piping to the seamline to find out how much fill should be

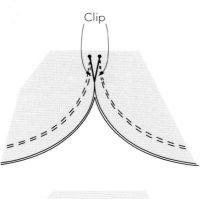

Clip

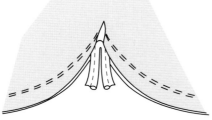

cut off. Pull the bias strip back while holding the fill, exposing the fill. Cut the fill off at the measured distance and pull the bias strip back over the cut end.

Then, clip the seam into a "triangle" on both layers. Turn the piece right side out. With a bodkin pull the ends of the piping through the opening between the ends of the seams to the wrong side.

5. To finish the inside corner, stitch across the base of the "triangle" catching the ends of the piping in the stitching. To ensure a crisp, sharp angle, hand-tack the pipings at the corner, pulling the pipings together.

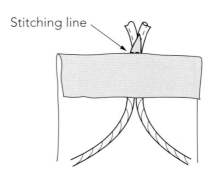

Stitching line

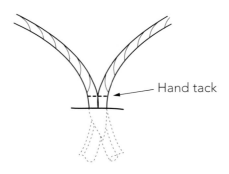

Hand tack

COMPLEX PIPED SEAMS WITHIN A PATTERN PIECE

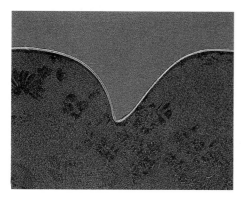

Sometimes there is a complex piped seam within a garment piece, such as a sharp angled seam, that is difficult to construct in the usual way.

1. In this case, baste the piping to the right side of the fashion fabric and stitch with the foot in Position #2, since this is regarded as a final seam. Once the piping is sewn in place, trim and clip the seam allowances and press them back against the piece.

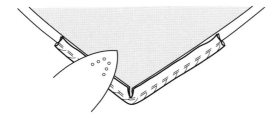

2. Baste the two pieces together, lining up the cut edges of the seam allowances.

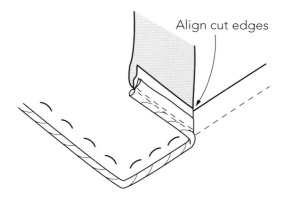

Align cut edges

3. With an edgestitching foot, stitch-in-the-ditch where the piping is sewn onto the piece.

DOUBLE AND TRIPLE PIPING

A single row of piping is nice, but an edge can be enhanced with double and triple piping. Multiple pipings can be made by just stitching a number of pipings together, but people might pull them apart and see the stitching lines and say "tsk, tsk!"

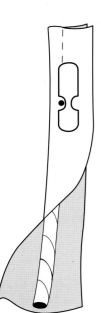

1. Cut and stitch bias strips together for all layers of piping in the usual manner, but cut the strips at least ½" wider than usual. You can always trim later if necessary. The first row of piping made will be on the top edge, the last one will be nearest the seam.

2. Make the first layer of piping in the manner described in "Basic Piped Seams," with the zipper foot in Position #1.

3. Then, sew the second layer bias strip to the first finished piping, with the zipper foot in Position #2 (this is a final seam). By making the layers of piping in this way, the stitching line will not show in the finished product.

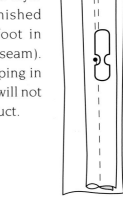

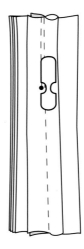

4. To fill the second bias strip, flip over the piping piece and place the zipper foot back into Position #1 and sew, creating the second layer of piping.

5. To add a third layer of piping, follow steps 2 and 3 above. More layers can be added, but after three pipings flexibility is hampered, so curves are not as easy to negotiate. Straight lines are best for a piece of more than three pipings.

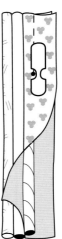

Now, you ask, how do you put a backing onto this? There are two methods, both of which involve handwork. The dreaded handwork, you say! Really, sometimes it's faster and easier than using the machine!

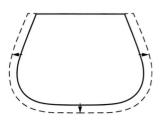

For the first method, cut the facing with the seamline pushed outward to match the extra width added on the piped edge by the multiple rows. The rule of thumb is add an extra ⅛" for each additional row of piping. Hand stitch the seamline on this piece to the outermost row of piping.

The second method involves piping the facing piece with a piece with one less row of piping. For example, if triple piping is used, pipe the facing with a double piping, and then hand sew this to the front piece. The outermost row of piping on the piece will form the point, as shown below on a cross-section of the edge.

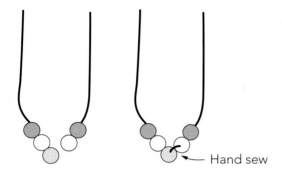

— Hand sew

To join the ends of the piping around a garment or other piece, try to plan the design so some embellishment will cover the join. Joining may not always be possible such as on circular pieces where the piping goes all around the edge. If that is the case, pull back the stitching holding the strips together and join the individual bias strips, making sure the seams align (just like piping a pillow). Trim each piping fill and finally stitch in the order of construction.

PIPED POCKETS AND BUTTONHOLES

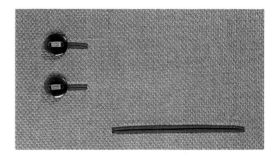

Now that you have an understanding of this method of piping, the piped buttonhole and pocket are next. You will use the ¼" adjustable zipper foot and you will quickly see why you must have this particular foot.

1. When marking for a piped pocket or buttonhole, first, on right side of fabric, establish the center line of the opening and the length markings. Next, mark a line a scant ¼" (more like ³⁄₁₆") parallel to the opening line. This is the piping placement line.

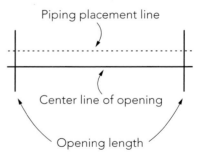

Piping placement line

Center line of opening

Opening length

Next, if interfacing is desired (if the opening is on the bias), use a double layer of organza, running the lengthwise grain parallel to the opening. If the buttonhole is being made in a garment that has interfacing under the area of the buttonholes, make the buttonholes in the fashion fabric layer only. Cut openings into the interfacing to accommodate the buttonhole. Whipstitch the seam allowances of the button-hole after the interfacing is installed. This reduces bulk later.

2.   Cut two pieces of piping, each 1½" longer than the desired opening. Lay the filled section of the piping along the placement line leaving ¾" at each end for finishing. Place the zipper foot in Position #2 and start stitching at the opening point with a short stitch length of 0.3–0.5 mm. Stitch for ½" with the short stitches, then lengthen the stitches to 1.0–1.2 mm. Line the piping up with the placement line while stitching the piping. Shorten the stitches again ½" before the end and stop on the end mark.

3.   Trim the seam allowance of the piping to ⅛".

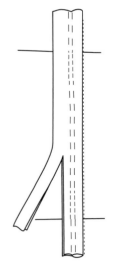

4.   Before the second piece of piping is stitched down, trim its seam allowance to ⅛". Starting at the same end as before, shift the foot so the needle is on the oppo-site side of the zipper foot and in Position #2. Stitching in the same direction will prevent the pocket from looking "twisted" when finished.

Place the piping under the foot, and push it as close to the first piping as possible. Lower the foot between the two pipings; it will push them apart the required distance.

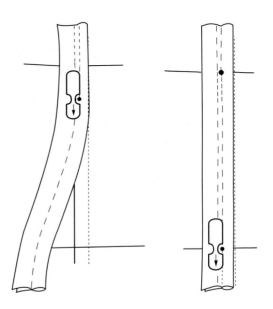

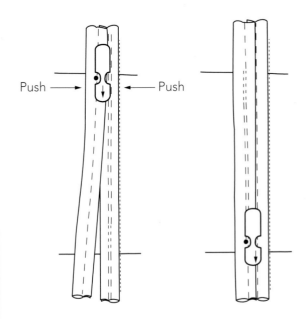

Push →   ← Push

While stitching, keep the right edge of the foot tight against the piping already sewn, and push the two pipings together as you stitch along the second piping. The foot is exactly the width of the opening, and will keep the two pipings parallel. Shorten and lengthen the stitches as in step 3. Both lines of stitching should begin and end on the end marks.

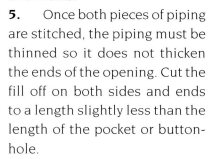

5. Once both pieces of piping are stitched, the piping must be thinned so it does not thicken the ends of the opening. Cut the fill off on both sides and ends to a length slightly less than the length of the pocket or buttonhole.

It is at this point that the piped buttonhole and piped pocket techniques diverge. The next section refers to the piped buttonhole technique. The piped pocket will follow.

6. On wrong side, cut the opening by making a small slash, and clipping to the ends of the stitching, forming triangles. If you make this type of buttonhole often, invest in a pair of very sharp embroidery scissors just for this task.

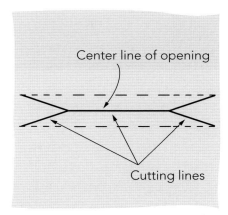

Center line of opening

Cutting lines

7. Turn right side out, making sure the ends of the opening are square by lying the piece flat. Baste the piping pieces together with silk thread. The silk thread will leave no marks when pressing. To finish the ends, fold the fabric back onto the opening at the end, perpendicular to the opening line. Pull the triangle of fabric over the ends of the piping and stitch across the ends with very short stitches using the zipper foot.

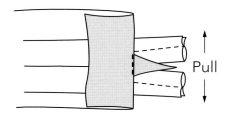

Pull

For best results in pressing, use the seam roll, and place the piped buttonhole or the piped pocket opening parallel to the roll and press. This will ensure that no impressions of the seam allowances will mar the appearance of the fashion fabric.

TIP

By trimming the rattail fill from the piping, there won't be excess bulk in the ends and the fabric in the opening will fold back just where it should. Then by using the zipper foot, the line of stitching falls right where it is wanted, without disturbing the placement of any parts. Make sure the piping pieces meet in the center and don't overlap. One way to ensure this is to pull the ends of the piping apart just before stitching and then release. Both ends are done the same way.

8. The buttonholes are kept basted closed until the facing is attached. Once attached, mark the placement of the openings for the buttonholes by inserting pins at the ends of the buttonholes and then marking the opening on the right side of the facing. This can be done either with chalk or by basting.

Create an oval shaped opening in the facing piece. Draw a line between the marks extending this line by ⅛" on each end. The extra measurement at each end compensates for the loss of length when making the oval opening. If this is not done, the buttonhole will be too tight for the button. Draw a narrow oval about ³⁄₁₆" wide. to be used as the stitching line.

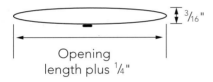

³⁄₁₆"

Opening
length plus ¼"

9. Place a piece of organza on the right side of the facing piece, and stitch around the drawn oval. The stitch length is 0.5–0.7 mm. Slash the oval open, turn the organza back through the opening, and press. If there is interfacing in the facing piece, whipstitch the organza to it; if there is none, baste the organza with silk thread to secure until the buttonhole is finished.

10. Finish the buttonhole by hand-sewing the facing opening to the back of the piped buttonhole.

Piped buttonholes can be nonfunctional as well. A line of decorative buttonholes along the edge of a garment is quite an exquisite trim. In this case, after the buttonhole is turned and finished, the opening is whipstitched closed from the back and no openings are cut in the facings.

The outer ends of piped buttonholes can be embellished with a combination of decorative buttons and metal ends for a very beautiful look.

Piped buttonholes and piped pockets can be curved as well as straight in design. To achieve this, the curve of the opening is drafted first, along with the end marks. A second parallel line is drawn the same distance as for a straight opening (scant ¼"). The first piping is sewn along this line, the seam allowances are trimmed, and the opening is finished in the same manner as a straight one. This is how the "smile" pockets on western wear are stitched.

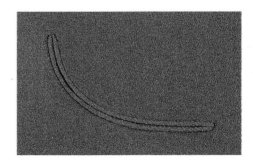

PIPED POCKETS

Construction of the piped pocket begins in the same manner as the piped buttonhole, except it is obviously longer. When drafting a pocket opening onto an existing pattern, the rule of thumb is the pocket openings should be no less than 6" in length. This provides room for the hand to get into the pocket. I prefer an opening of 6½" or 7" for women's garments and 7½" or 8" for men's.

1. When stitching a piped pocket, marking and steps 1 through 5 are the same as for the piped buttonhole, above. Interfacing rules apply here also. Once the pipings are in place and the rattail has been trimmed back, the pocket bag is placed.

There are two types of piped pockets, horizontal and vertical. For the vertical, the opening is marked on the pocket piece after cutting, and is pinned into place over the pipings on the right side of the fabric, matching any markings.

For the horizontal pocket, the bag is created by cutting a rectangle twice the desired depth of the pocket (you will prefer at least 8", for a total of 16" of length) plus 1" for seam allowances. The width is the length of the opening plus 2". Align the center of this rectangle onto the pipings, right sides together.

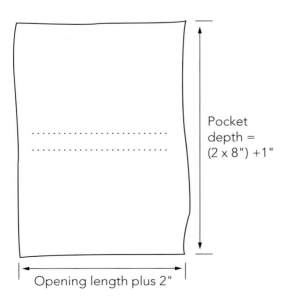

Pocket depth = (2 x 8") +1"

Opening length plus 2"

2. Turn the piece over so the stitching lines are visible. With the zipper foot in Position #2, stitch again along both piping stitching lines. When stitching, the zipper foot will travel between the two stitching lines (and the two pipings). A short stitch length of 0.5–0.7 mm will be used. For this operation the zipper foot can be left in one position and the work can be turned to stitch in the opposite direction.

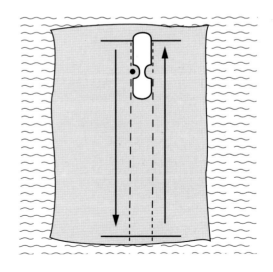

3. Once these lines have been stitched, slash the pocket layer and the fashion fabric separately, as is done for the buttonhole, leaving the "triangles" at the ends.

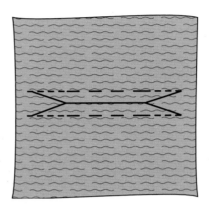

4. As the ends of the piping have already been thinned, pull the bias cover ends to the back through the space between the stitching lines at the pocket ends with a large-eyed needle.

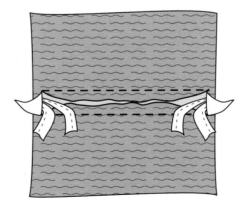

Turn the pocket right side out through the opening. Baste the pipings together with silk thread, making sure the ends are square. Press using the seam roll.

5. Stitch the ends of the opening using the same procedure as is used for the buttonhole. Be sure the ends of the piping meet but don't overlap.

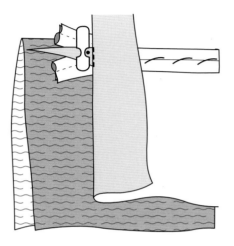

6. To finish the pocket bag:
For a vertical pocket, pin on the other half of the pocket and sew together, using the desired seam finish.
For a horizontal pocket, press both sides of the pocket bag toward the bottom of the piece. Pin the lower "lip" of the pocket opening to the upper "lip" and lay the piece flat on the table. Smooth into place and continue pinning the pocket bag together.

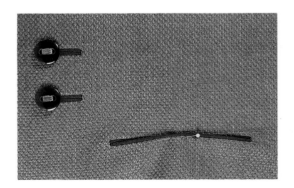

Stitch the pocket bag with the zipper foot, starting ¼" to ½" from one end of the pocket opening and finishing at the other end. Pink or serge the seam allowances of the pocket bag.

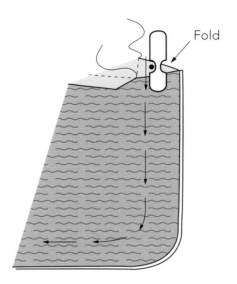

Pinning the lower "lip" to the upper "lip" shortens the back half of the pocket bag in relation to the front, thereby relieving the tension that makes the pocket gape open.

Curved, or "smile" pockets are sewn and finished in the same manner. But the pipings are stitched on a curve before the pocket bag is placed.

As with the buttonhole, the ends of the pocket can be embellished with beads or other interesting items. Placement of these pockets in multiples is most attractive, as is embellishing the ends with bias tubing made from the same fabric.

FUN TRICKS WITH PIPING FOR THE HOME

A nifty piping trick is using organza for the bias cover and decorative cord as the fill. This is particularly attractive for home furnishings and is useful when applying those cords that don't have a flange. Use this sheer cover when the cord has a tendency to fray, as the organza keeps it tidy, or when a slightly darker color is desired, as a black organza cover cuts the color quite nicely. Prepare the organza bias strips as usual and make the piping using the above methods for the piping construction.

Two methods for making knots in the piping are also fun and especially nice for the corners of Turkish cushions. The first is the proper, labor-intensive method, and the second is the "cheater's" way for those times you need to get it done quickly, for whatever reason!

1. When making piping for knotting, use the thicker, upholstery weight fill and your adjustable zipper foot. To determine the width of bias strips to cut, wrap the fabric snugly around the fill, mark on each side of the fabric, and then add two times the desired seam allowance. Cut and piece the bias strips in the usual way. Assume two times the length needed to go around the piece to account for the amount taken up by knotting. When stitching the fill into the piping for this operation, use a normal stitch length of 2.0–2.5 mm, as a secure seam is needed here. After the piping is made, begin by thinning the end of the piping by at least 2"–3". Baste the piping on, beginning where the fill was removed, as the excess cover will be used in finishing the ends later. Baste up to the place where the first knot is desired.

2. Tie the piping into a knot, marking on the seamline where the piping goes into (A) and comes out (B) of the knot. This will determine the length of piping used in each knot.

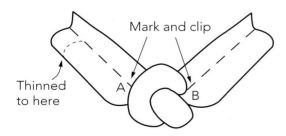

Mark and clip

Thinned to here

A B

3. Untie the knot, and trim the seam allowances down to ⅛"–¼" between the marks (A & B). Staystitch the seam between the marks (A & B) with a short stitch length of 1.0–1.5 mm to reinforce.

A B

After stitching and trimming, tie the knot again in the piping, adjusting it so the seam allowance is hidden in the knot. Secure the knot with some hidden hand-stitching.

4. Baste the piping down along the seamlines, stopping to form knots at each desired point. The last knot will conceal the beginning of the piping. Be consistent when tying, so all knots present a uniform appearance. After tying the last knot, thin the piping as was done at the beginning. Baste this end to the beginning end, concealing the seam in the knot.

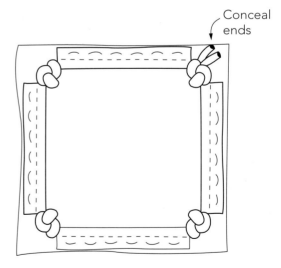

Conceal ends

5. Stitch the piping down with the zipper foot in Position #1. With right sides together, pin and stitch the final seam with the foot in Position #2. Trim all seams and press. Once the seams have been sewn, the knots should be secured with hand stitching to keep them in position.

So now, what's the cheater's way?

Again, measure the distance around the piece plus a few extra inches for one length of piping needed. Make and trim a second length of piping (see step 3 above).

1. Begin by tying a knot in the second piece of piping to determine the knot length needed. Add 1½"–2" at each end for finishing. Based on this measurement, cut the number of pieces of piping needed for the knots. Thin out the ends 1½"–2" at each end of each piece.

2. Beginning at the point of the first knot, thin out the end, and baste the first piece of piping down along the seam to the first knot. Staystitch the seam allowance a length sufficient to accommodate the knotted piping and trim the seam allowance to ⅛"–¼". This will make a gap where the piping will not be stitched into place. Using one of the pieces of piping you prepared, knot it around the piping, making sure the ends will fall into the seam.

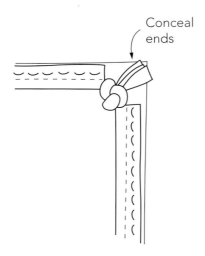

Conceal ends

By just wrapping the piping around the piping twice and running the ends into the seam, you can create a different look.

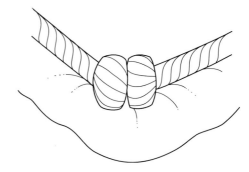

3. Continue around the piece in the same manner and finish by concealing the ends in the last knot. Machine stitch the piping down with the zipper foot in Position #1. With right sides together, for the final seam put the foot in Position #2 and sew. As with the knotted piping above, some hand-stitching should be used to secure the knots into position.

Another trick with piping is what is called "strap piping." This is a piping made with two or more fills in one cover. It looks really cool around cushions.

As with the other pipings, this piping is made with bias fabric. The width is two (or more) times the distance around the fills, plus two times the seam allowance, plus ¼" for ease. The length is the measurement necessary to get around the piece with some to spare for finishing.

1. The first fill is put into the fold of the bias strip and stitched with the foot in Position #2 (this is a final seam). Lay the next fill (and any subsequent ones) between the layers of the cover, right up against the previous one, and stitch with the foot in Position #2. A contrasting decorative thread in the needle would be appropriate here.

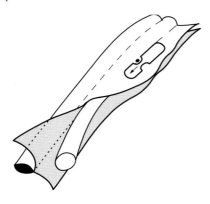

TIP

When installing strap piping into a piece, there are some things to know. In rounded pieces, this type of piping tends to lie flat when constructed flat. If a round flange effect is desired, first press the bias strip in half, then press it into a curved shape. Stitch the fills in while keeping the bias cover in the curved shape. Make sure you cut the cover on the wide side, to allow for clipping and a more controllable seam allowance, as well as adding some extra length.
  When using unshaped strap piping around a cushion or other piece, the seam appears to be off-center unless the two halves of the piece are favored to compensate for this illusion. Be sure to favor the seam.

---

2. Join the ends by first removing the stitching a short distance from the ends. Sew the bias cover together at the ends. After trimming and pressing the seams, cut out the first fill so the ends butt together and complete the first seam with the foot in Position #2. Cut and finish the other ends in the same way.

PIPING AND FILLED BIAS TUBING COMBINED

Another cool trick with piping is to combine piping and filled bias tubing in one length. This is really nifty in home furnishings for things like drapery tiebacks, or making a semi-fitted slipcover that ties to fit, the tie being the piping. Some planning is required, especially if a length of piping with both ends finished with bias tubing is desired.

1. Prepare the bias strips as usual. Determine how long the tubing will be at the end. Make it much longer than necessary, as it is easier to cut off the excess rather than add on later. Staystitch for about 1" along the seamlines of the bias strip at the point where the tubing ends and the piping begins. The staystitching reinforces the seam for this transition from tubing to piping. Make a clip in the seam allowance on each side.

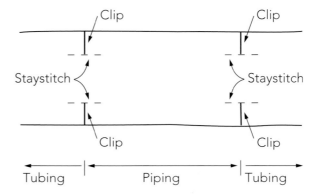

2. With right sides together, sew the bias strip up to the clip, making the tubing, using a stitch length of 1.0–1.5 mm. Place a cord into the tube to the end and sew across the end. Trim the seam allowance to ¼". Whipstitch the fill to the seam allowance at the end. Pull the tubing right side out, working the cover over the fill. Those bias tubing devices are really helpful here!

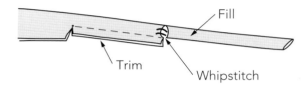

3. Once the tubing is turned right side out with the fill inside, make the piping by setting the fill into the fold of the cover and stitching. Stitch along the staystitching lines when starting the stitching. Stitch with the foot in Position #1 and make piping as before.

4. If another tube is desired at the end of the piping, there is a different construction order. Determine where the piping will end and the tubing begins, and mark. Staystitch along the seamlines of both edges at this point to reinforce. Note that the tubes can be filled first, then the piping seamline can be sewn.

TIP

Keep in mind, bias strips stretch, so when measuring lengths it is best to measure the fill then stretch or shrink the cover to fit. This will make for a more accurate finished piece.

POCKETS

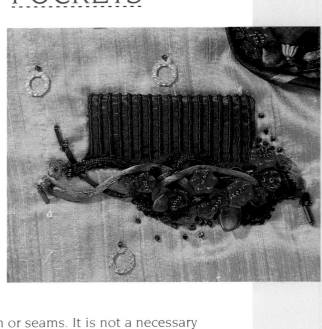

DEFINITIONS

• **Pocket Bag:** The part of the pocket that actually holds the contents of the pocket. For the pockets outlined here, except for the lined patch pocket, the pocket bag is a separate pattern piece.

• **Pocket Lining:** The inside piece of a patch pocket, not to be confused with the pocket bag.

• **Welt:** The part of a set-in pocket that stands up from the opening seam or seams. It is not a necessary part of a set-in pocket.

• **Opening:** Place where the hand enters the pocket.

Pockets can be very loosely categorized as either set-in pockets or patch pockets. Patch pockets are just what the name implies, a patch that serves as a pocket. The set-in pocket is inserted into a seam or into the body of a piece and has an opening and a separate pocket bag.

LINED PATCH POCKETS

This blindhem pocket application is especially nice when a patch pocket without topstitching is desired. The finished look is very clean and is best on tailored clothing. Suggested fashion fabrics for this type of pocket application are wool crepe, wool sateen, any tweed, melton, or other suit weight fabric. Lining fabrics can match the lining of the garment, or organza can be used if a lighter weight is desired on a pocket that will not receive much use.

1. Draft the pocket with a 1" facing folded back for the top edge. The lining piece is drafted to join to the facing and is favored ⅛" smaller than the pocket piece. Favoring causes the seam to fall to the back when the pocket is sewn and pressed, so it is not visible when the pocket is installed.

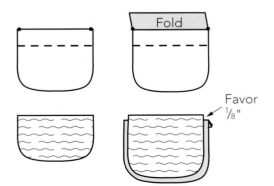

2. With right sides together, sew the lining to the facing edge, leaving an opening of about 2" for turning. Press seam allowances toward the lining.

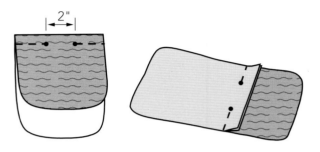

3. Align the edges of the pocket, pin, and sew. Trim the seams and clip the curves. Turn the pocket right side out through the opening, and press. When pressing, make sure the seam falls to the back side. Slipstitch the opening.

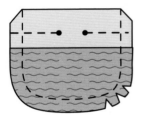

Machine Settings—Sewing Machine
Stitch: Blindhem
Stitch Width: 0.6–0.8 mm
Stitch Length: 1.0 mm
Presser Foot: Adjustable Zipper Foot

4. Pin or baste the pocket into place on the front of the garment piece. Position the zipper foot far to the right so it sits over one of the rows of feed dogs and move the needle position to the right one notch.

5. When starting to stitch, secure your stitches with the securing function on your machine. If your machine doesn't have this function, shorten the stitch length to zero and make a few stitches. As you are stitching, pull the fabric of the pocket to the left to expose the seam where the lining is attached. The adjustable zipper foot enables you to see exactly where the needle is without impeding the action of the stitch. Stitch all the way around the pocket, and at the end use the securing function to end the stitching. Do a final press.

> **TIP**
>
> The zigzag of the blindhem stitch takes a small bite from the lining fabric. The short stitch length makes the stitch take bites closer together for a more secure attachment. Test before sewing to make sure that the needle can swing as close as possible to the foot without striking it. You will notice that since you stitched to the lining and favored the pocket, all the stitching falls under the pocket piece and is concealed.

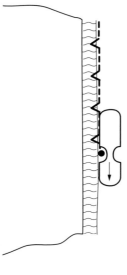

FOOLPROOF WELT POCKET

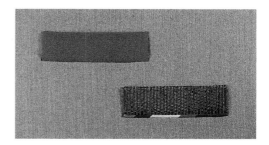

This welt pocket, constructed using the adjustable zipper foot, is a variation on the industry method of making a welt pocket. With welt pockets there is a tendency for the pocket lining to show when the pocket is at rest. This is the kiss of death! By using this method, the opening through which the pocket is turned is very narrow, which minimizes the show of the pocket lining when the pocket is either at rest or in use.

> **TIP**
>
> A rule of thumb for a pocket opening length is 6"–6½" for women, 7"–7½" for men. Pockets can be longer, but these measurements are the minimum for ease of use for most people.

1. To prepare the pattern, decide how deep the welt will be (at least 1"–1½"), and double this amount. The top edge is a folded edge which needs to be marked. The width of the welt is at least the minimum opening width. Now, add seam allowances to this pattern piece and it is ready to use.

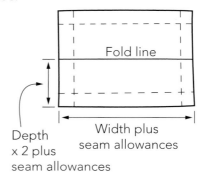

Fold line

Depth x 2 plus seam allowances

Width plus seam allowances

2. In commercial patterns the pocket bag is usually cut in two pieces, but this method is different. The pattern for the pocket bag is one large rectangle, saving time. The length is twice the desired pocket depth, usually 8" to 9", plus 2". The width is the width of the welt plus 2", the same as the piped pocket. The opening will be stitched in the center of this piece.

3. Cut the welt out of the fashion fabric, laying the welt pattern piece so the length is on the crosswise grain. The crosswise grain has more stretch than the lengthwise and will help in favoring later. Cut a piece of polyester, silk organza, or any other lightweight woven interfacing fabric, the same size as the welt with the foldline (top edge of pocket welt) on the lengthwise grain. The lengthwise grain has the least degree of stretch and will prevent the edge from sagging over time.

4. Press the interfacing piece along the foldline and place on the back side of the welt piece, lining up the foldline of the interfacing with the foldline of the welt piece. Edgestitch along the folded edge. This will reinforce the pocket edge preventing sagging. If extra reinforcement is desired, stitch a piece of twill tape at the top edge of the interfacing.

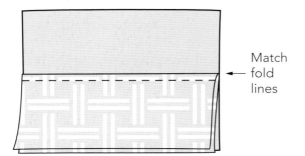

Match
fold
lines

5. Sew the side seams of the welt. Favor toward the outside by ⅛" at the base of the welt, tapering to nothing at the top edge. Pin, and sew along the seamlines.

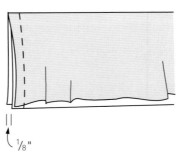

⅛"

6. Grade the seam allowances and clip the corners. Press, stretching the front of the welt slightly to enhance the favoring effect.

> **T I P**
>
> As discussed before, favoring allows you to control where the seams will fall. With the welt pocket, you want the seams to fall toward the back of the welt, so they won't be visible from the front once the welt is stitched into position.

7. Pin the finished welt to the center of the pocket bag piece, and baste. Starting exactly at the end, stitch along the seamline with the zipper foot in Position #1, and with the stitch length shortened to 0.5–0.8 mm. Sew with short stitches for ½", then lengthen the stitch to 3.0 mm. Stitch the seam until the last ½", then shorten the stitches again. End exactly at the end of the welt.

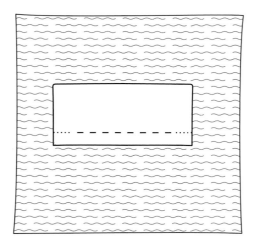

8. Trim the seam allowance of the welt to ¼", then taper the ends to almost nothing at the ends of the seam. This narrow seam allowance will help you make the very narrow opening which was mentioned earlier.

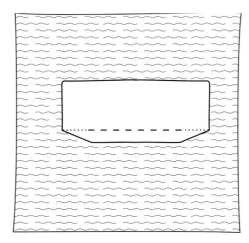

9. Lay the pocket piece down onto the right side of the garment, with the welt facing downward. If interfacing is desired for the pocket opening, it is attached beforehand.

There will be a seamline visible on the pocket piece. Measure up and over from the edges of the piece, using this seamline for correct positioning of the pocket. In this way, you need not have X-ray vision to position a pocket. Baste in place along the stitching line, making an extra tack at each end to secure.

10. With the zipper foot in Position #2, follow the stitching pattern diagrammed. The foot is first positioned to the right of the needle, when stitching from A to B, pivot the fabric while stitching from B to C, and C to D.

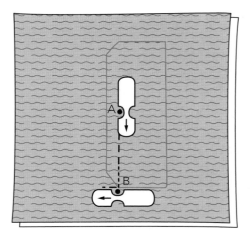

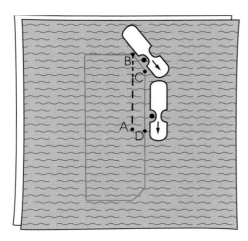

The needle is raised at point D, the foot is shifted to the left of the needle and moved to point A, where sewing proceeds to point E, then pivoting to point F. Here the foot is moved back to the right of the needle (still in Position #2), and the rest of the seam is sewn to point D. When turning the corners at points B and E, it is especially important to hold the welt down with a point turner. The additional thickness of fabric makes it want to roll, causing the seam to fall short.

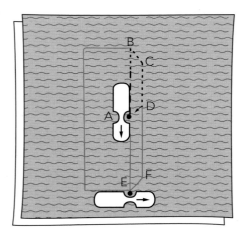

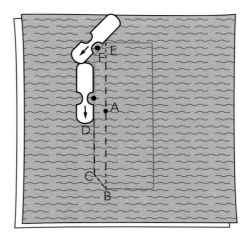

11. At this point, check your work before cutting. If, despite your best efforts, you get a gap at the corner of the welt (it does happen—don't panic!), simply turn the entire assembly over and go over the corners again, making sure the zipper foot is snug against the welt. Your stitching line should be closer in toward the welt than the other stitching line, correcting this gap.

You are working from the center of the welt to the sides, so you don't have to jump up onto the welt at the corners; you drop off the ends. Shortening the stitches at the ends keeps the corners from bursting after clipping, and angling in at the corners causes the seamline to fall behind the welt and be invisible.

TIP

Remember when stitching the corners to walk the machine one stitch at a time when coming to the corner. Stop at the end of the welt! The needle will sound and, if you are hand-turning the flywheel, feel different when it has reached the end. It will now be going through only the fashion fabric and pocket bag. You stop when you hear (or feel) the first stitch that is different. If you are in doubt, pull the pocket piece up and look to see if the needle is at the end of the welt.

If you go past the end of the welt, there will be a little gap at the end. Most unattractive! Use your point turner to hold the sides of the welt down against the bed of the machine as you are walking up to them. Otherwise, the fabric has a tendency to slip out from under the foot, causing the seam to be slightly away from where you want it.

If, after you have stitched the opening, you spread the layers apart and find that the stitching is not as close as needed (it also happens!), turn the work so the other side is facing up, and stitch in the same manner. Make sure you now have everything snug under the foot, and stop at the ends of the welt.

12. After the stitching is complete, *and you have checked your stitching,* cut the opening. Slash the pocket layer first, then the garment layer. Cut "triangles" into the corners of the opening after the two layers are cut. Pull apart slightly. When clipping the corners, appliqué scissors work very well. The fulcrum is more forward, giving power and control, and the thick spines at the back of the blades keep the points together when going through thicker fabrics.

13. Push the pocket through the opening. From the back, press the upper seam allowances and the welt seam allowances downward. The sleeve board is helpful here. Turning over to the front, steam and block-press the welt seam allowances downward.

14. To form the top of the pocket bag, fold the garment piece back at the ends of the welt, and pull the pocket piece to the side, making sure that the fold of the pocket bag occurs in line with the top seam. Press.

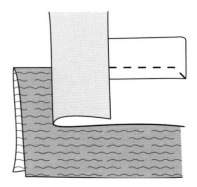

15. Pin the pocket bag together, and stitch around the piece with the zipper foot, keeping the side seams close to the ends of the welt. Either serge or pink the seam allowances to finish.

16. Attach the welt back to the garment by hand stitching from the back of the piece. Start at the base of the welt and catch the seamline of the welt with each stitch. Go to the top of the welt, then reverse the stitching, ending at the point where you began. In this way, no stitching will be visible from the right side of the garment.

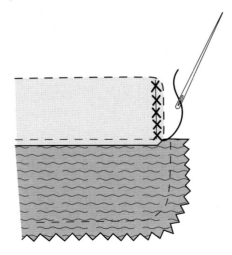

PIPED WELT

Sometimes piping is desired when making a welt pocket. The order of constructing the welt changes slightly in this case.

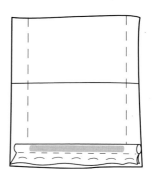

1. When making the welt itself, after the interfacing is stitched to the back side of the welt, piping is basted and stitched to the front half of the welt along the seamline. After stitching with the zipper foot in Position #1, thin the piping so it doesn't get caught in the side seams. Once this is done, the side seams of the welt can be constructed in the usual manner.

2. After the welt is constructed, sew it onto the pocket piece with the zipper foot in Position #1. By basting the welt to the pocket piece, the welt is kept from "rolling," a tendency it has when piping is used. Baste along the seamline. Lengthen and shorten the stitches as usual and trim and clip the seam allowances as above.

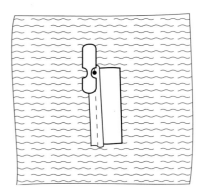

3. The stitching pattern and order are different than for the unpiped welt. Follow the steps diagrammed, shifting the foot to the right of the needle at point B and to the left of the needle at point F.

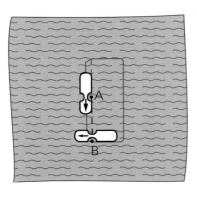

Move foot to right of needle

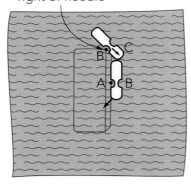

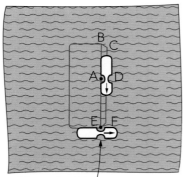

Move foot to left of needle

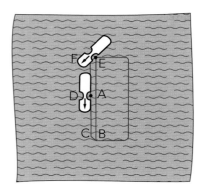

4. Clip, turn, and finish the pocket in the same manner as the unpiped welt.

HIDDEN-LINING POCKET

When you line a jacket (which is almost always), make the lining as one unit and hand-attach it to the inside of the jacket once all the facings and hems are stitched down. A pocket inside a jacket is an essential. This hidden pocket is not only functional but it's attractive as well—and for those who worry about pickpockets it's both invisible and difficult to pick. An advantage to this type of pocket

is that, if the jacket needs relining, there is no pocket attached to the facing to work around, which simplifies things considerably. Also put your label into the pocket, it's much more tasteful than displaying it on the back of the neck.

1. To draft this pocket onto an existing garment pattern, pin the facing and lining front pieces together at the seamlines. Mark where the opening is desired, and use the same measurements mentioned above regarding pocket opening length. Only seamlines are shown here. Add seam allowances later.

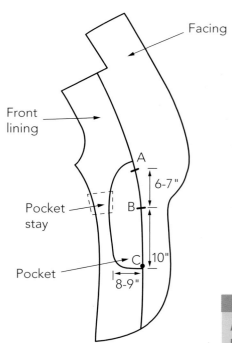

2. After marking the opening and seamline of the pocket, transfer the markings to the facing piece, and trace the pocket piece onto fresh paper, adding the desired seam allowances.

> **TIP**
>
> A tip on pocket placement, especially on women's jackets—make sure that the opening is at or slightly below the bust, and the depth is enough so that the contents of the pocket rest below the bust, not on it.

3. To construct the pocket, first construct the lining in its entirety. Baste filled piping to the seamlines where the lining joins the facings. Stitch the piping in place with the zipper foot in Position #2 (this is a final seam).

4. After cutting the pocket pieces from a suitable fabric and marking the notches, pin one half of the pocket to the lining, right sides together, matching the marks. With the zipper foot in Position #2, stitch between points A and B, and clip at point B.

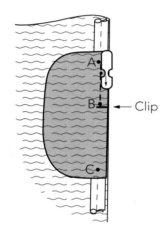

5. For the other half of the pocket, cut a piece of piping 1" longer than the distance between the notches. Baste the piping between the notches, and stitch with the zipper foot in Position #2 between points A and B.

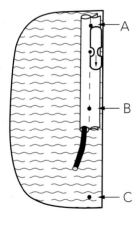

6. Pull the rattail fill completely out of the piping, clip as shown at point B, and press the seam allowances back. Removing the fill from the piping reduces bulk, while providing an attractive finish when attaching the pocket to the facing.

7. To pin the two halves of the pocket together, first lay the piece flat. Align the piping on the back half of the pocket (the one with the fill removed), slightly inside the piping stitched to the lining edge. Pin the pocket together with the pieces aligned, and stitch the seam from A to C.

8. Turn the entire pocket assembly so the pocket and right side of lining are together. With the zipper foot in Position #2, stitch the remaining open side to the piping on the edge of the lining, starting at point B and sewing to the bottom of the pocket, C.

TIP

By pinning the piping on the back half inside the front half, the back half of the pocket hides behind the edge when the pocket is in place.

9. Trim the seam allowances on the pocket piece to ¼" and press all the seam allowances toward the pocket piece.

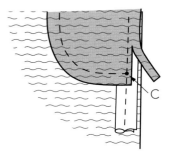

10. At the top of the pocket opening, stitch using a securing stitch to reinforce that end of the opening. Repeat the procedure at the other end. Finish by stitching all the seam allowances onto the pocket piece.

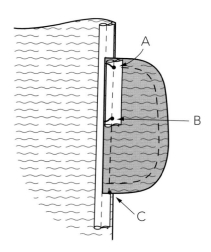

11. Create a pocket stay to keep the pocket from curling down into the inside of the garment and inhibiting the free motion of the hand into the pocket. One of two methods can be used. The easiest method is the "tack"—if the pocket crosses a seamline, tack the seam allowances of the pocket to the nearest seam allowance. Use the second method in cases where a seam is further away. Sew a strip of organza to the outside seam allowance and connect it with the nearest seam allowance. Organza is best because it keeps its shape while not thickening the piece. Polyester or silk organza are both suitable.

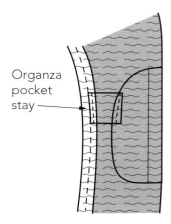

Organza pocket stay

12. Once the pocket is constructed, baste the lining into the garment and try it on your dress form before continuing. Any problems of improper placement will be discovered before the hand work is done. The hand stitch which attaches the lining to the garment is a simple running stitch. It first catches the piping just above the stitching line,

> **TIP**
>
> A tip on hand-sewing linings: Divide the lining stitching into four or five sections and knot off the thread at the end of each section. Be consistent in where the breaks occur in every garment. In this way, if you ever need to go back into a garment for repairs or adjustments, you only have to worry about cutting one section, and you'll know exactly where the stitching begins and ends.

then it catches the facing piece. When approaching the pocket, use the running stitch to the end of the pocket, then backstitch two or three times in place to reinforce the seam. Continue on by stitching the flattened piping on the back of the pocket with the same running stitch and, again, reinforcing with the backstitch. Continue until the end, as discussed above.

NIFTY HIDDEN-EDGE POCKET

This is a really nifty pocket and a variation of the hidden-lining pocket mentioned above. It is useful for lightweight piped edges when there is no other place to put a pocket. It is quite suitable for evening wraps.

1.   Draft this pocket pattern in the same manner as the hidden-lining pocket. Placement (below the bust, ladies!) is drafted onto the pattern, and openings are no less than 6" long. Draft a U-shaped opening for the pocket front, as well as a corresponding place where it will be attached to the body of the lining. The edge of the pocket is directly along the seamline. Draft the back of the pocket with a straight edge at the opening, which will ultimately become the seam allowance.

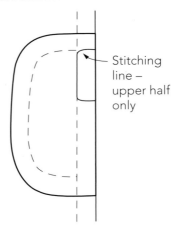

Stitching line – upper half only

2.   Stitch the piping to the body of the piece with the foot in Position #1. Stitch the front of the pocket to the lining along the "U"-shaped line. Use short stitches and a piece of silk organza cut on the lengthwise grain for stability.

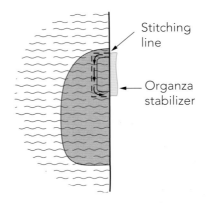

Stitching line

Organza stabilizer

Grade the seam and clip the curves, turn right side out, favor toward the back, and press.

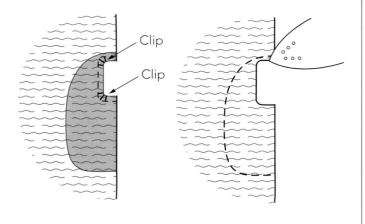

3. Sew the back of the pocket onto the front. The seamline where the lining is joined to the body of the garment is not sewn.

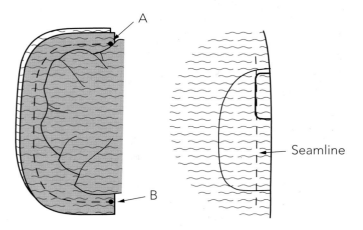

4. When joining the lining to the body, align the two pieces so that the sewn edge of the pocket opening is *right on* the piping sewing line. The pocket back forms the seam allowance which attaches to the body of the piece. Sew with the zipper foot in Position #2.

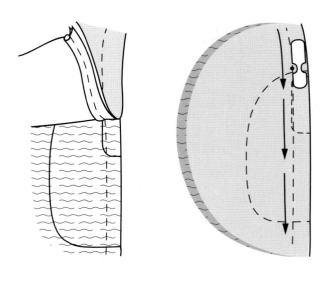

THE TAILORED SHOULDER

DEFINITIONS

- **Sleeve Cap:** The upper, curved portion of the sleeve that attaches at the shoulder seam. It is usually eased.

- **Sleeve Head:** A strip of padding inserted into the seam between the sleeve cap and body. It pads out the sleeve cap, eliminating any puckers caused from easing and creates a graceful appearance.

- **Shoulder Pad:** Also called a shoulder shape, this is inserted into the shoulder at the armhole to support and give shape to the shoulder and sleeve cap.

- **Shields:** These are reinforcing structures attached to the front body interfacing (and sometimes the half-back) that smooth out the dip between the collarbone and shoulder bone. Shields are not often used in relaxed tailoring.

- **Half-Back:** An interfacing piece for the back shoulder area which provides support for the fabric, as well as a place to stitch down the shoulder pads.

DRAFTING FRONT AND BACK INTERFACINGS

Commercial patterns usually have pattern pieces for the front body interfacing but not the back. Draft these interfacing pieces based on the information in the illustrations shown here. Seam allowances must be added.

1. Cut the front interfacing from the hymo hair canvas and a "thin cheap" fabric. These pieces are then handled in the same manner as outlined in "Treatment of Interfacings Not Stitched into Seams" in the opening chapter, "Before Beginning." When this unit is stitched into the seams of the garment during construction, the seamline will fall ⅛" away from the cut edge of the canvas, and just the "thin cheap" fabric will be caught into the seams. The seam allowance will pad out the difference.

2. The interfacing front is familiar to most, but the half-back is new to some. This piece is cut from cotton batiste or another thin woven fabric, and is put in as a back interfacing piece which takes strain off the fashion fabric when the garment is worn. An advantage to the half-back is that it provides a foundation on which to stitch the shoulder pads. This prevents the pads from curling (they will!) and "showing-through" on the outside of the garment. If a really built-up shoulder is desired, shields can be made for the back as well and attached to the half-back.

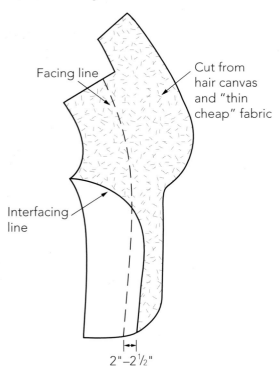

Facing line

Cut from hair canvas and "thin cheap" fabric

Interfacing line

2"–2½"

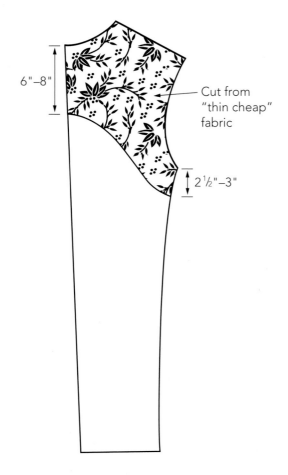

6"–8"

Cut from "thin cheap" fabric

2½"–3"

SHIELDS

1. Draft the patterns for the shields, front and back as shown. They are drafted onto the existing interfacing or half-back pattern, and then traced off onto fresh paper.

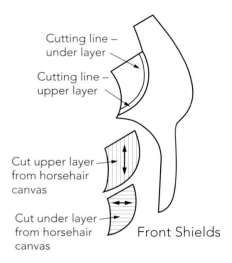

Cutting line – under layer

Cutting line – upper layer

Cut upper layer from horsehair canvas

Cut under layer from horsehair canvas

Front Shields

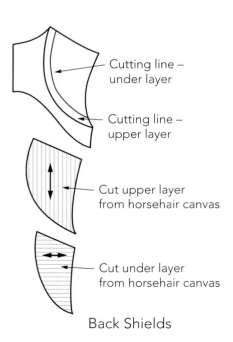

Cutting line – under layer

Cutting line – upper layer

Cut upper layer from horsehair canvas

Cut under layer from horsehair canvas

Back Shields

2. Stitch these pieces by machine to the back of the interfacing, the side closest to the body when wearing.

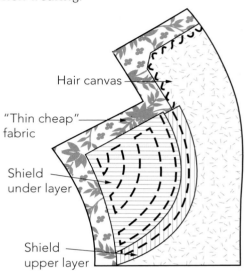

Hair canvas

"Thin cheap" fabric

Shield under layer

Shield upper layer

SLEEVES

When drafting the sleeve pattern, allow no more than 1"–1¼" of ease in the cap, the optimum is 1". If there is more, remove it by either lowering the cap by ⅛" increments, or by slashing the pattern from cap to cuff and folding out the excess. The slashing and folding method works for those patterns where the sleeve cap is traditionally too low to begin with. In general, use the slash and fold method rather than lowering the sleeve cap.

Slash and overlap

Add

Add

LININGS

Make the entire lining before installing it into the jacket. Some modifications are necessary.

1. Check the sleeve cap height of the lining in relation to the body piece (points A to B). It should be about ½" lower to accommodate the shoulder pad.

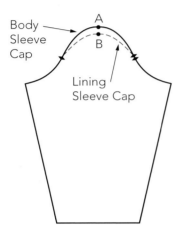

2. Lower the shoulder line (points A to B) at the armhole slightly, ¼" front and back, to compensate for the pad. This will keep the lining from bunching at the shoulder.

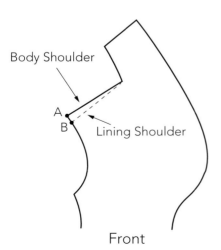

Front

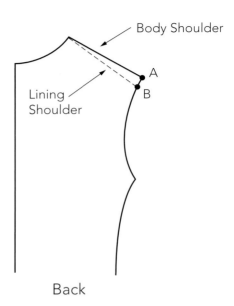

Back

SHOULDER SHAPES INCLUDING THE FLAT SHOULDER PAD

When making jackets with set-in sleeves, you need a shoulder pad. Thank heaven we got past that period in fashion when men's jackets went without. Everyone just looked frumpy!

There are two types of shoulder pads, set-in and raglan. As you will see when you purchase shoulder pads, there is an astounding variety to choose from. The set-in pads fall into two broad categories, nonwoven (including the foam pads) and stitched.

The nonwoven pads are usually covered with a pellon or synthetic felt fabric, with the filling—foam or synthetic fibers, and sometimes cotton—fused to the pad. Some pads have really stiff coverings, and are just the thing to have when making shoulders that will clear off shelves in department stores!

These pads can be different thicknesses, but my favorite is about ½" thick with a compact cotton fill fused to the pad. They tend to be firm, and to increase the thickness you can stack more than one pad together.

The stitched pads are covered with either pellon or woven cloth, and are filled with cotton or synthetic batting, which is stitched together by hand or machine with *big* stitches. These pads tend to be softer, and need to be pressed over a ham before installing. The advantage to this type of pad is that you can take it apart to add or remove filling to customize the pad. If you are filling out a shoulder pad, use cotton batting, pressing it into layers before adding it to the pad. Once the desired thickness is achieved, stitch the pad together with big stitches that are secure but not tight. Start in the center of the pad and work outward in rows, shaping the pad over your hand as you go. If you build in the shape while sewing, the pad will hold its shape for the life of the garment. Always press the pad over a ham before installing.

Occasionally you may wish to make a tailored coat with no added height at the shoulder. In this case, what is needed is a pad that supports the shoulder with no padding. This is done with layers of interfacing fabrics.

1. For the pattern, use any tailored shoulder pad to get the outline and shoulder notch. Draw two lines (B + C) ¾" away from one another, inside the outline (A), as shown. Trace three shoulder pad pieces on fresh paper following these lines. Cut layer A on the bias from hymo canvas. Cut layers B and C from hair cloth with the hair running as indicated by the arrows.

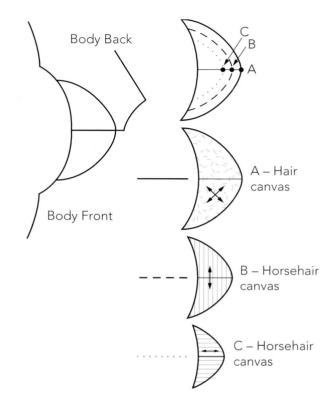

A – Hair canvas

B – Horsehair canvas

C – Horsehair canvas

Horsehair braid

2. Stitch the layers together by machine with parallel rows of stitching running ½" apart. Stitch a piece of ½"-wide horsehair braid, the length of the shoulder pad, to the armhole edge with two or three rows of straight stitching. The horsehair braid keeps the edge true after assembly, otherwise the weight of the sleeve cap could cause the sleeve to ripple.

If this pad is installed as a traditional pad it will ripple, so you need to install it in a different manner.

3. Place the garment on the dress form and position the pad in the garment. The edge of the pad will extend, at most, ½" into the sleeve cap. After pinning the pad to the garment, baste it securely in place along the armhole seamline and outer edge of the pad while the garment is still on the form. Once basted, the shoulder pad can be stitched into place. First, stitch the armhole edge to the sleeve cap seam allowances, and then tack the outer edge.

EASING THE SLEEVE CAP

Once the sleeve is cut out and constructed, easing is done. The method described here is a variation of the "lambswool" method from *Power Sewing* by Sandra Betzina Webster, but here you will use loosely-woven wool mohair fabric. This fabric is more expensive than lambswool, approximately $80.00 a yard, but you can buy ⅜ yard and get quite a few sleeve heads from it. The wool mohair is preferable to silk mohair, as the silkier fibers find their way to the outside of the piece.

With this technique, you will install the sleeve head and ease the sleeve in one operation, saving time.

1. Cut the strips of mohair on the bias, 3" wide and 1½" longer than the distance between the ease notches on the pattern. Place the strip 1" past the easing notch, lining the edge up with the seam allowance on the sleeve. Starting at the easing notch, stitch a few stitches ⅛" in from the actual seamline (½" seam allowance).

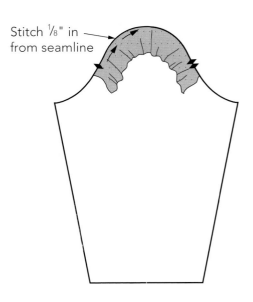

Stitch ⅛" in from seamline

Stretch the strip as much as possible while sewing the strip down all along the sleeve cap, ending at the opposite easing notch. The stitching line will remain ⅛" in from the seamline all along the way.

2. Trim off the strip at the other end so it is 1" past the easing notch, and shake the sleeve. The ease will automatically come, and will be even. The mohair will not cave in as readily as cotton sleeve heads, and will fluff-up with steam. This treatment will eliminate those annoying puckers that form on the sleeve cap.

3. Install the sleeve into the armhole as usual. Baste before sewing to check the fit. An advantage to basting is that the layers can be held in their final relative positions, so that the whole garment can be run through the sewing machine any direction that is convenient. After trimming and clipping and so forth, the shoulder pad can be added in the usual manner. Steam the entire shoulder *after* the pad is in place, holding it over your hand and letting it hang as it will when worn. When your hand is scorched, you know it's pressed!

DESIGNER EMBELLISHMENTS FOR HOME AND APPAREL

DEFINITIONS

- **Flange:** Refers either to a strip of twill tape functioning like the seam allowance on piping that is stitched to a decorative cord or trim allowing it to be sewn into a seam; or it is a flat border sewn into a seam that stands out of the seam perpendicular to the surface of the fabric when viewed in cross section.
- **Knife Pleat:** A pleat or series of pleats that lie flat, one over the other.
- **Accordion Pleat:** A pleat that looks like a zigzag when viewed in cross section.

Knife Pleat

Accordion Pleat

- **Mushroom Pleat:** Also referred to as the "Fortuny" pleat, this pleat is created by knife pleating the fabric, and then box pleating over the knife pleats. Fabric can be bought this way or sent out to a commercial pleating establishment to achieve this effect.
- **Crystal Pleat:** A very tiny accordion pleat, either purchased or commercially created.
- **Prairie Points:** Squares of fabric folded into a triangular shape and used as edge trim.

PARTS OF THE PLEAT

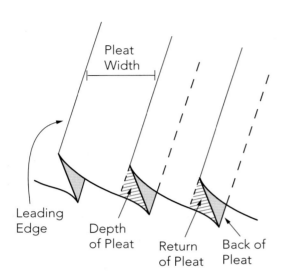

- **Leading Edge:** This is the crease on the front side of the pleat. On the outer side is the pleat width, on the under side the pleat depth. It's reversed on the back of the pleat.

- **Pleat Width:** The portion of the pleat which extends from the folded edge of the pleat to the fold of the next pleat.

- **Depth:** The part of the pleat that is concealed when the pleat hangs correctly. It is two times the pleat return.

- **Return:** The distance from the fold at the leading edge of the pleat to the back of pleat fold.

- **Back of the Pleat:** The fold at the center of the pleat insertion, usually not seen unless it is an accordion pleat.

KNIFE-PLEATED EDGE

For this edge you will use ribbon or fabric cut on the straight of grain. To find the length of ribbon needed, measure the seam to be embellished and multiply the measurement times three.

TIP

Length times three is the best way to figure fabric needed for gathering, whether it's for curtains or skirts. Two times is skimpy, and two and a half is harder to multiply. Another reason to use "three times" is an old theater trick—you can get away with using cheap fabric if you use more of it when gathering.

The width of the strip used depends on whether you want to use ribbon or prefer to make the strips out of regular fabric. Select a ribbon wide enough to stand out of the seam with enough left over for seam allowances. When using fabric, determine how high the edge will stand out of the seam, preferably ½" to ⅝" wide, add a seam allowance, and multiply by 2. The strips will be pressed in half before pleating.

Once the strips are cut, either use one of the pleating devices on the market (for small amounts, this is dandy) or send the strips to a pleating house. When sending them out, be sure to tell them not to cut the strips into sections but pleat in one continuous length. Joining them together later is not fun, make no mistake about it!

1.   To attach a knife-pleated edge to a piece, first, baste the pleated edging to the piece and stitch with the foot in Position #1. When basting and stitching, *be sure the edge of the pleating is perfectly parallel to the seamline!* If it's not, it will look really bad. Basting and stitching (Position #1) will secure the edging so it doesn't move.

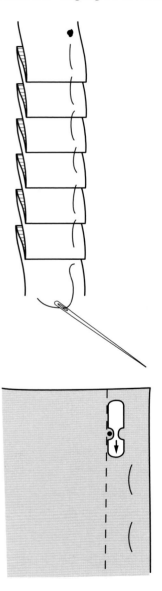

2.   To finish the seam, with right sides together, position the other piece on top of the edged piece. Pin, and sew the seam with the zipper foot in Position #2.

Now, if despite your best efforts the edge of the pleating does *not* lie perfectly parallel to the seam (it happens!), don't despair. Don't rip either. Once the piece is done, tack each corner down with a bead. This makes quite a nice edge and camouflages crooked work.

PLEATED RUFFLE

The pleated ruffle is easy to make and looks like a million bucks. Start with the fabric already pleated, either with a tiny knife pleat, crystal pleat, or mushroom pleat. Stiffer fabrics work better for this technique, taffeta for example, but other fabrics are also appropriate.

To determine the cut width of the prepleated fabric, add the width of the desired ruffle, plus ½" to ⅝" seam allowance for one edge and ½" for the other edge for finishing. The length of the strip is the length of the seam it goes into, *plus* one third. For example, if the seam is 10", the strip will measure 13" long. You want extra fabric in the seam so the edge will create more "sweep."

There are two ways of finishing the edge and both use monofilament thread—you know, fishing line! A good weight for this purpose is 20-lb. test, big game line, bought at sporting goods stores. Bring your own spool, as this stuff is sold in bulk and is wound directly onto the fishing reel.

1. The first way to finish the edge is the easiest. Use a serger 3-thread rolled hem and a cording foot. Quick, tidy, and efficient.

However, there are some of you who don't own a serger, but you can just use your sewing machine. It's a little more time consuming but worth the effort.

Machine Settings—Sewing Machine
Stitch: Zigzag
Stitch Width: 0.6–0.8 mm
Stitch Length: 4.0–5.0 mm

2. Since you added ½" to the edge for finishing, first, pull the fabric flat and press a "bend" ½" in from the raw edge along the edge to be finished.

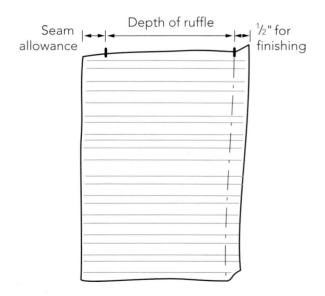

3. Place this "bend" under the presser foot, with the crease down on the throat plate. Zigzag the monofilament into this "bend." The "bend" forms a valley that the monofilament falls into.

Machine Settings—Sewing Machine
Stitch: Zigzag
Stitch Width: 0.6–0.8 mm
Stitch Length: 0.5–1.0 mm (satin stitch)

4. Trim the excess fabric close to the monofilament, taking care not to cut the stitches. The "bend" will now roll over the monofilament. Overcast the edge with a satin stitch, adjusting the width to cover the monofilament. The "bend" helps the satin stitch cover the "pokeys" (fabric threads that poke out of the satin stitching), because the edge rolls over the monofilament.

The needle should fall off the edge of the fabric on one side of the work. If the monofilament isn't covered on the first pass, run the piece through the machine a second time.

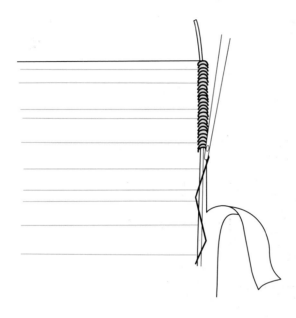

What do you do with the ends of the monofilament? Since the ruffle has sweeps and curves, I stitch the ends of the monofilament into the seams; aesthetically this works well and saves aggravation.

This process can also be used on a nonpleated fabric to make a ruffle. The three-times rule still applies for the length of the strip. Finish the edge before ruffling, then ruffle the fabric strip with either a ruffler attachment or using other machine gathering methods. Stiffer fabrics are better here, too, as the ruffle tends to fall back onto itself with limp fabrics. By prepleating the fabric, a sort of "boning" effect is created with limp fabric, keeping the ruffles erect.

PRAIRIE POINTS

This is a quilting technique adapted for clothing by reducing the scale of the prairie points and adding a flange.

1. Cut your strips as diagrammed, making them any width you desire, but a good starting point is 3"–4" wide. This width makes a petite prairie point, suitable for clothing, but larger strips can create quite a lovely effect for home furnishings.

2. Fold the cut strip as shown below, with the back side of the fabric facing up. Press as you fold. When using striped fabric, the direction of the stripes will alternate, which is quite a cool effect.

1.

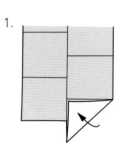

2.

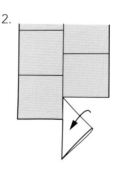

3.

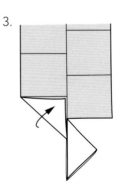

4.

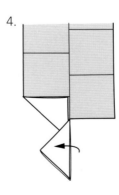

5.

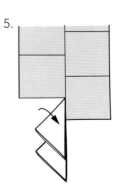

3. Once the strip is folded and pressed into place, stitch the whole piece to a 1" bias strip to provide a flange for sewing it into the garment. This cleans up the edge and reduces the bulk going into a seam.

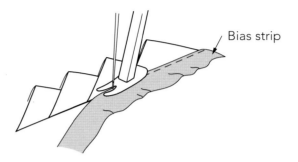

Bias strip

4. Baste the strip into the garment after the piping is sewn in. Then stitch with the foot in Position #1 (not a final seam). The seam is then constructed as usual, trimmed, and pressed. As a nifty touch, the points of the edge can be tacked down with a bead for more interest. This elegant technique works nicely when edging something such as a footstool.

CHINESE KNOTS AND FROG CLOSURES

Chinese knots and frog closures are other embellishments that can be used for both apparel and home furnishings. In home furnishings, they are quite effective as tiebacks for draperies, as well as closures for slipcovers. A really tasteful treatment is to use them on a center back opening of a chair slipcover. It's an easy way to elevate a mundane slipcover to something memorable.

Any type of cording or bias tubing can be used for these knots and closures. If you are working on a project where cost is an issue, buy less expensive fabric and put your money into the cord for the trimming. This will elevate the entire project.

The Chinese knot is tied as diagrammed here. Once the basic knot is mastered, it is pulled and massaged into the round shape of the knot. Another use for this knot sequence is for a frog closure. The knot is tied in the same way but pulled out flat, as opposed to rounding it. This makes a very nice frog.

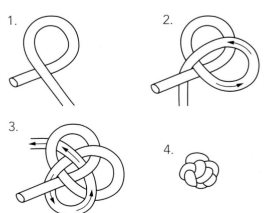

FINISHING TOUCHES

DEFINITIONS

- **Mold:** Piece of wood or other material that gives shape to the "knob" of the tassel. The fringe of the tassel hangs from the mold, and the mold can be either covered by the fringe or covered by other materials.
- **Knob:** The rounded part of the tassel attached to the cord.
- **Waist:** Found below the knob and above the skirt, the indented section of the tassel that looks like a "waist."
- **Skirt:** The loose strands of fringe that provide the movement to the tassel.
- **Chainette Fringe:** The name of the fringe used when making the tassels. It is rayon, comes in lengths from 2"–30", is available in a wide range of colors, and takes dye easily if color matching is desired. The fringe ends are chainstitched with contrasting thread for shipping and this thread is removed before working.
- **Foundation:** Rows of chainstitching joining the individual strands of fringe.
- **Seed Beads:** Round-shaped beads available in a variety of sizes.
- **Bugle Beads:** Tubular beads that are measured by millimeter.
- **Home Row:** The first row of beads, usually seed beads, that the mesh cage is built from.
- **Nymo Thread:** Spun nylon thread that is as strong as dental floss. This is the "Timex watch" of thread, and you should use Nymo exclusively for bead mesh. It is sized by letter, size B being a good all-purpose size. For best results, iron the thread before use, as ironing will take out the twist and make the thread less prone to knotting.
- **Working Above the Fabric:** Refers to working only through the holes in the beads to create certain effects. In bead mesh, after the home row is attached to the piece, the needle travels only through the holes in the beads. It doesn't stitch into the tassel at all.
- **Unit:** The bugle-seed-bugle beads sequence that is strung onto the thread. Ultimately these units make up the mesh.
- **Point:** The seed bead in the middle of the bugle-seed-bugle unit. The seed beads actually form a point when they are the uppermost row, and later form an intersection in the mesh.

PARTS OF A TASSEL

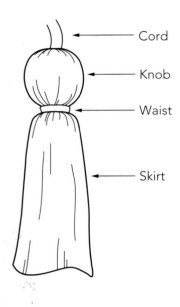

Cord

Knob

Waist

Skirt

PARTS OF FRINGE

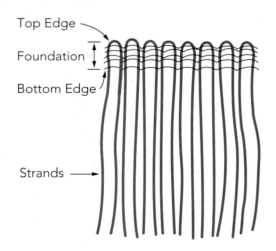

Top Edge

Foundation

Bottom Edge

Strands

Rayon chainette fringe is readily available at most notions counters. Using fringe for tassels saves you the trouble of wrapping cord around a card or board and tying one end, since it's already secured by a foundation, and the individual strands will not shed over time. Also, fringe is easy to control while constructing tassels.

Since the fringe comes in lengths from 2" on up to around 30" you can make any length of tassel desired. The longer tassels are easier to construct with fringe, as you have more control over the materials. Using this method of tassel construction, it is easier to add a tassel to finish a tie or cord on a project. Think how nice these tassels would look finishing some of those piping techniques discussed earlier!

SINGLE-LAYER TASSELS

When constructing a tassel, the thickness of the tassel depends on how much yardage of fringe is used. For our purposes here, we will discuss tassels made from 16" of chainette fringe that makes a tassel with a knob approximately 1¼" thick.

1. First, make a knot in the end of a piece of cord to mount the tassel. This will keep the tassel from pulling loose. Whipstitch one end of the fringe foundation to the cord above the knot, positioning so the strands are pointing back towards the cord. The tassel will be wound upside down.

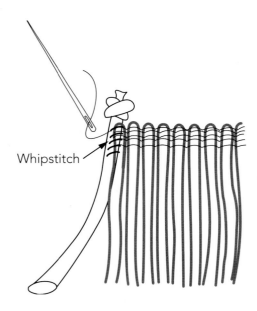

Whipstitch

2. Roll the fringe foundation snugly around the cord, making sure the top edge remains even, and resting against the bottom of the knot. Once all the fringe is rolled, whipstitch the remaining end of the foundation to the roll. Take several stab stitches through the roll of foundation, making sure the needle also passes

through the cord. This will secure the fringe so it doesn't pull away later.

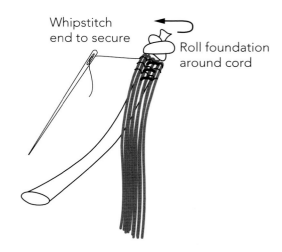

Whipstitch end to secure

Roll foundation around cord

3. Rethread the needle, attaching it to the bottom edge of the rolled foundation. Tightly wrap the thread many times around the strands of the fringe just below the bottom edge of the foundation. This pulls the strands tightly against the cord. The thread will then "fall off" the roll of foundation as it should. Take a few stitches to secure and knot.

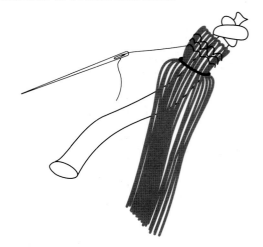

4.   Take a couple of stitches through the knot in the cord with a rethreaded needle. This keeps the cord knotted over time. Do not remove the needle and thread at this point. Turn the tassel right side up by holding onto the cord. The strands will now fall over the roll of foundation, concealing it. Evenly distribute the strands around the tassel with a blunt needle or one of those plastic hair lift combs. Pull firmly down on the strands to set them.

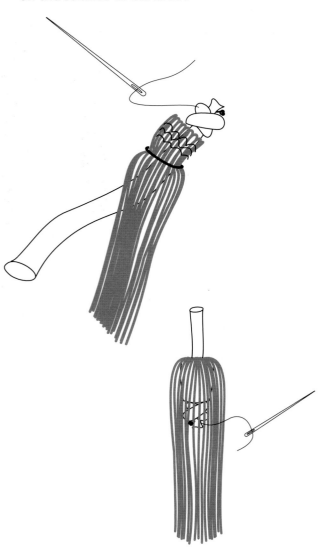

5.   To form the waist of the tassel, you may wish to attach the other end of the cord to a "third hand," or have someone hold the tassel for you. The needle and thread are still attached to the knot and will be hanging down among all these strands. Bring the needle to the out-side, and, with one hand holding the strands below the knob, wrap the thread around once. Pass the needle under the thread where it starts, and then wrap it several times in the opposite direction. Stitch and knot to secure. This change in direction when wrapping prevents a dent in the waist where the thread exits the strands.

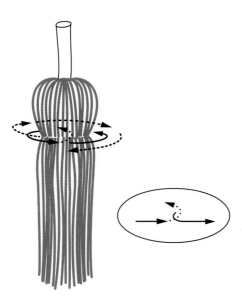

6.   After the waist is closed, you will want to conceal the thread at the waist by covering it with beads. After rethreading the needle, or using a beading needle, depending on the size of the beads used to cover the waist, pull the needle and thread up in the center of the skirt

(A), exiting on the waist (B). The knot will be concealed in the skirt.

7. String onto the needle and thread as many beads as necessary to go around the waist of the tassel. Pull the beads around the waist, and then pass the needle again through the first bead on the strand (A). Pass the needle through the tassel at the waist, coming out on the opposite side of the waist. Pull the thread snug but not tight, otherwise a dip will be created on the waist. Whipstitch over the strand of beads to keep it from falling off the waist, making sure the stitches fall between the beads. To finish, knot off and cut the thread.

> **TIP**
>
> When putting beads around the waist of the tassel, use a 5/0 seed bead. This bead is about $1/8$" across. For the tassel discussed above, you will need 20–22 beads. Use even numbers when making the home row.

DOUBLE- AND TRIPLE- LAYER TASSELS:

This variation on the basic tassel method uses multiple layers of different lengths of fringe, which are attractive in different colors. Each layer is numbered from the longest (bottom) layer up, with the last layer attached before forming the knob called the top layer.

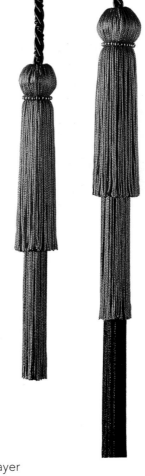

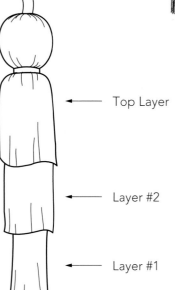

← Top Layer

← Layer #2

← Layer #1

Layer #1 is wound on first, with succeeding layers wound on top of this one. On the single-layer tassel, you used 16" of fringe to create a 1¼" knob. For this operation, you will use a *total* of 16" of fringe, only it will be divided between the layers.

For double-layer tassels, layer #1 has 7" of fringe, the top layer has 9". For triple-layer tassels, layer #1 has 3", #2 has 5", and the top layer has 8" of fringe. Notice that the under layers have less fringe, and the succeeding upper layers have more. It takes more fringe to cover the circumference as the tassel gets thicker. More fringe around the upper layers guarantees coverage and balance.

1. The cord is *not knotted* for this tassel. Attach the fringe, layer #1, by first stitching the end of the fringe to the cord, rolling it up, then stitching the end to secure. The under layers of fringe are attached with the strands facing the direction they will hang when the tassel is finished. This is the exact opposite of making the basic tassel. Attach all but the top layer by winding them directly on top of fringe layer #1 and then stitching the ends securely.

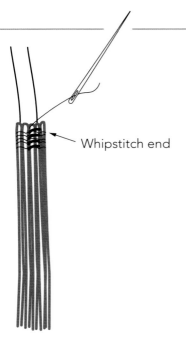

Whipstitch end

2. Stitch the top layer onto the rolled foundations of the other fringes, but with the strands facing the opposite direction. Roll the top layer of fringe and stitch in place.

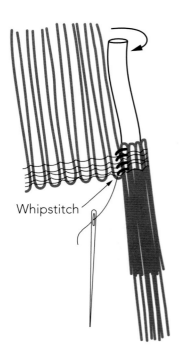

Whipstitch

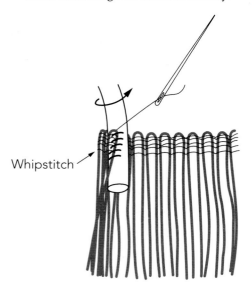

Whipstitch

Rethread the needle and wrap the strands so they are snug against the cord, just as you did in the single-layer tassel. Stitch to secure, and knot off.

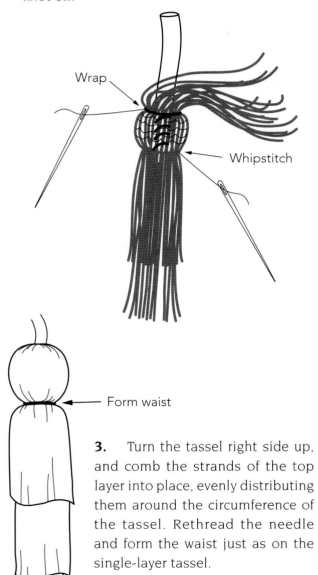

Wrap

Whipstitch

Form waist

3. Turn the tassel right side up, and comb the strands of the top layer into place, evenly distributing them around the circumference of the tassel. Rethread the needle and form the waist just as on the single-layer tassel.

TRIMMING THE TASSEL

Rayon chainette steams out really well. After the tassel is completed, steam the tassel with your iron, and shake it to let the strands hang out. Even up the ends by simply cutting them straight across with scissors. For multiple-layer tassels, trim the top layer, and work down by pulling the other layers aside while letting the layer to be trimmed hang alone.

With multilayer tassels, trim layer #1, $\frac{1}{4}$"– $\frac{3}{8}$" longer than the other layers to make it appear to be the same length. This is one of those optical illusions where if all layers were the same length, layer #1 would look shorter than the upper layers. When making tiered skirts, the bottom tier is made $\frac{1}{2}$" wider than the upper tiers for the same reason.

BEAD MESH

Bead mesh "cages" are quite nifty for covering the knob of a tassel. If a mesh cage is desired, a sample should be made before working on the final tassel to test bead sizes and appearance. The following guidelines will get you started.

1. Attach the home row of beads according to steps 6 and 7, "Single-Layer Tassels." Rethread your needle with a 36" strand of doubled thread of the Nymo. Bead mesh eats up thread, so give yourself *lots* of extra. Pull the needle up through the skirt of the tassel and come out on the waist, as you did when applying the home row, but come out between two of the beads (A).

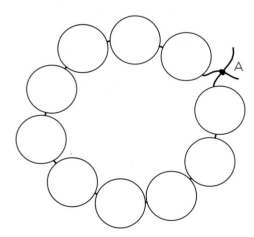

2. Thread one bugle bead, one seed bead (these can be any size, but the teeny ones work well for bead mesh. Experiment!), and another bugle bead creating a unit. Since you are working above the fabric now, the needle will pass through two of the beads in the home row. Therefore, the need for even numbers of beads.

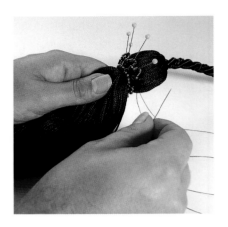

These units can then be pinned up onto the knob with straight pins to assist in shaping the mesh and keeping thread tension correct.

Bring the needle out between the beads and string another unit onto the thread. Pass the needle through the next two beads in the home row, and continue around in this manner until you arrive back at the starting point (A).

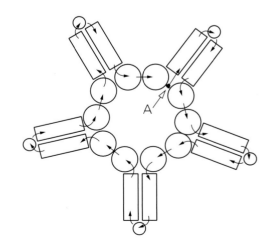

3. To move to the next row, after the needle exits the last two beads on the home row at the starting point, pass the needle through the first bugle bead (B) and the seed bead (C) in the unit (see illustration). From the seed bead (C), string another unit of beads on the thread. Then pass the needle through the next seed bead (D). Repeat this sequence all the way around. When working around the tassel, pull the pins from the first row to pin up the units of the second row. This means that you only need a few pins to do the job.

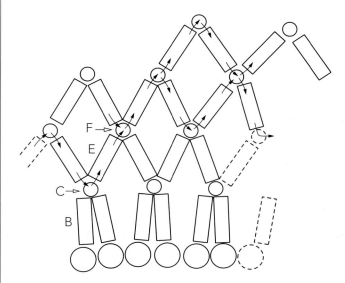

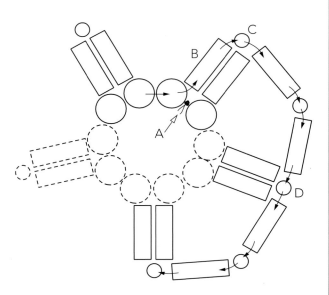

4. Move to the third and subsequent rows by passing the needle through seed bead (C), bugle bead (E), and seed bead (F). From there, add the next row of units, passing the needle through the "points." Be sure to keep moving the pins up as work progresses to avoid confusion as to which seed bead to pass the needle through.

TIP

To avoid confusion, the points on the uppermost row form an upside-down "V," which means "Very good, you may continue." The points not to use form an "X," meaning "No! Don't use this one." It's hokey, but it works.

5. To finish the mesh after covering the knob, draw up the last row like a drawstring bag to close the "cage." After moving to the last row, instead of using a "unit" of bugle-seed-bugle, just one seed bead is strung onto the thread. This seed bead can be either one of the same beads as the home row or one of the same beads as the "points." Pass the needle through the next point, another seed bead strung, and so forth until arriving back at the beginning of the row. Pull the thread, drawing up the mesh.

To secure, run the needle twice through the last seed bead, and then knot-off onto the thread of the mesh.

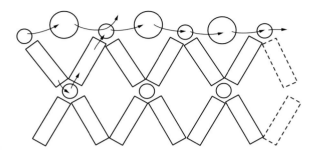

ADDITIONAL TASSEL EMBELLISHMENTS

With multiple-layer tassels, the upper layers can be tied into a series of tassels that look nice against the contrasting color of the lower layers. Braiding on the upper layers of a tassel, or making braids on the basic tassel, is also cool.

Many things can be used as tassel molds—thread spools, macramé beads, baby's teething beads, even actual tassel molds (when you can find them and then if you can afford them). With macramé beads, or other wooden shapes, the thing to look for is large holes. Molds can be part of the tassel or can be slipped onto the cord after the tassel has been made.

Two techniques for covering molds are **wrapping** or **upholstering**. Interesting effects can be achieved by wrapping the mold with ribbons, cords, or even beads threaded onto thread.

1. When using ribbons and cords, just keep passing the element through the hole, and either overlapping or butting up the element to cover the mold. A few stitches to tack the ends will finish the mold.

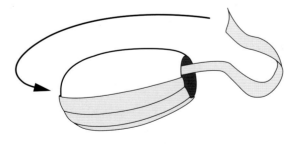

2. When using beads to wrap, just pass the thread itself through the hole, putting beads onto the thread to cover the outside. One less bead on every other strand helps to distribute the bead strands evenly around the mold. Bead mesh cages can be made to go around molds, or can be made to go around large marbles for a cool effect.

Upholstering a mold works best when used in combination with other techniques. Since not much fabric is usually required, this is a good use for scraps of that expensive fabric you have been saving.

1. Measure the circumference of the mold and the length of the mold to make a pattern for the casing. Add a little extra for seam allowances (½" on each side is plenty; you can trim later). Cut this piece out of the fabric, *on the bias*, unless you wish a stripe to travel around the piece. Bias fabric will finish better around the contours of the mold.

2. Sew the side seam, slip the cord into the casing, passing the cord through the mold, and secure.

3. Sew a running stitch to the end of the casing closest to the mold. Draw the casing up around the cord. Stitch the casing to the cord to secure. Pull the casing right side out and down over the mold. With a needle and thread, draw up the ends of the casing, tucking the seam allowances into the hole of the mold.

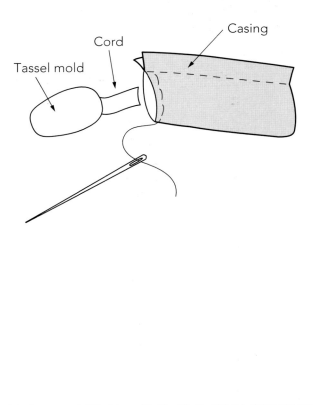

Casing

Cord

Tassel mold

CONSTRUCTING HANDBAGS

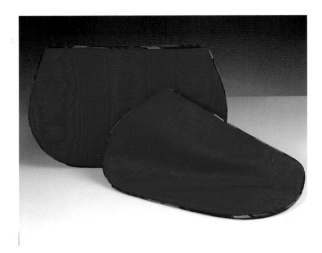

I will cover two types of piped handbag construction techniques that I use in my work—hard, or rigid, and soft. The hard construction works well for handbags that need a definite structure to communicate a certain aesthetic. Sculptural shapes can be achieved with a little experimentation once the basic principles are understood.

The soft construction is used when a softer, less constructed bag is desired. Many people find this type of bag more usable and easier to construct. With its softer construction and greater flexibility, the wearer is able to put more into the handbag. If you understand the soft handbag construction techniques, you are just a short leap from constructing the cuff on the wrap shown earlier.

There are a few supplies that are particularly useful in handbag construction.

Two-Ply Buckram is actually two layers fused together—one layer of buckram and one layer of crinoline. The combined layers produce a product that gives good support to the hard handbag.

Webbed Boning is normally used in strapless garments, but it's useful to "stay" the opening edges of the soft bag. The opening edges, which are stitched onto the boning, are then stitched directly onto the inside of the handbag piece without creating a casing.

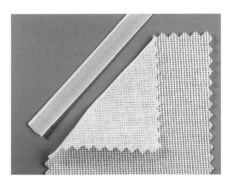

Curved Needles allow you to stitch fabrics to flat hard surfaces, as well as inside curves such as hat linings. No sewing studio should be without them. If they are not available in your area, try the local medical supply—surgical needles are a good substitute. Using curved needles takes a little practice, so don't give up until you master them. You will be rewarded for your diligence!

> **TIP**
>
> The most common source of curved needles is in the "repair packs" sold at most fabric store notions counters, but other finer needles are also available. The one to request is the #2 curved needle. Comparable in diameter to a regular sewing needle, its curve is similar to that of a half-dollar.

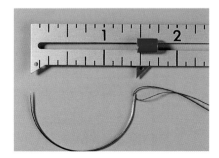

Another term often used in handbag construction is the gusset. A gusset is an additional fabric piece inserted into a seam which provides extra room and a greater range of movement for the wearer. In handbag construction, a gusset enables the maker to create interesting, three-dimensional shapes.

DRAFTING THE PATTERN

Different patterns are needed for the different types of handbag construction. The process of drafting the handbag and lining patterns for both types of bag is outlined here. The illustrations were drawn without seam allowances, which you will add after drafting your pattern.

1.   For both bag styles, draw a vertical line in the center of your paper. This line will be the center of the bag and the paper will be folded in half to produce two identical sides after one side is drafted. Draw a horizontal line perpendicular to the center line for the top opening of the bag. Handbag openings (A–C in both diagrams) should be no less than 3" (full width of 6"). Anything narrower will be inaccessible to the hand.

2.   For the soft bag: Draft the desired outline for the handbag (line A–B). Measure in ¼" from A to A' and ½" from B to B'. Connect A' to B' following the outline of the bag for the lining piece. Line A'–C is the opening for the lining piece. The lining is ½" smaller than the outer bag, eliminating any bunching at the corners when the lining is inserted into the finished handbag.

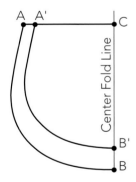

3.   Trace both the handbag and the lining pieces onto fresh paper and add the desired seam allowances to each piece.

4.   For the hard bag: Draft the desired outline for the handbag (line A–B). Measure down 1"–1½" from C to C' and draft a line perpendicular to the center line from that point (C') to the bag line (D). Measure in ⅜" from point D to point D'. Connect C' to D'. Line C'–D' is the lining opening. As on the soft bag, measure up ½" from B to B', and connect B' with D' to form the side seam of the lining.

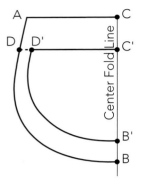

5. Trace the hard handbag pieces onto fresh paper, and ADD SEAM ALLOWANCES TO THE LINING PIECE ONLY. The handbag pattern is used as is, with no seam allowances added.

> **TIP**
>
> On the hard handbag, the opening edge is faced with a bias strip of lining fabric, and the opening edge of the lining starts 1"–1½" down from the opening of the bag itself.

Your handbag can be composed of many pieces, but to provide the easiest construction techniques, the process is explained with two halves-front and back. The instructions below can be easily adapted to projects with multiple pieces.

SOFT BAG CONSTRUCTION

1. Using the handbag pattern piece, cut two pieces each from the fashion fabric, the felt interlining, and "thin cheap" fabric for the front and the back. From the lining fabric, cut two lining pieces, one each for the front and back of the bag.

2. On the front and back sections, layer the fashion fabric over the felt interlining. Measure and make piping to fit the outer edge of the bag. Baste the piping down along the outside edges of one interlined piece, and stitch with the zipper foot in Position #1 (see "Piping for Apparel and the Home"). Baste and stitch piping to both opening edges using the zipper foot in position #1.

> **TIP**
>
> Piping is attached to the side of one piece only because when both halves of the bag are stitched together one piping should show. If piping is added to both pieces, there will be a double row of piping. If you prefer this effect, attach the piping to both sides, thin the ends (see "Piping for Apparel and the Home"), baste the piping along both edges, and stitch with the foot in Position #1.

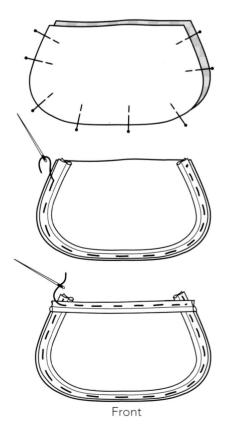

Front

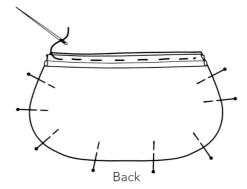

Back

3. With right sides together, place the front and back interlined pieces onto the "thin cheap" fabric, and pin. With the zipper foot in Position #2, sew around both pieces, ending the stitching by overlapping the stitching line by ¼" from where you began. When sewing the piped half, the zipper foot follows the visible line of stitching. For the other piece, follow the stitching line along the edge. Use the appropriate guideline on your sewing machine to keep the stitching lines straight.

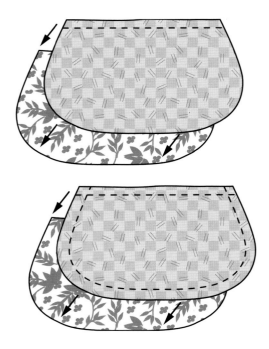

4. After clipping the curves and grading the seams (the felt is graded to ⅛"), cut a slash through the center of the thin cheap fabric. Turn both pieces right side out. Press and close each slash with a featherstitch. We now have a completely faced edge around each piece. From now on, the "thin cheap" fabric is just along for the ride as another layer of interlining.

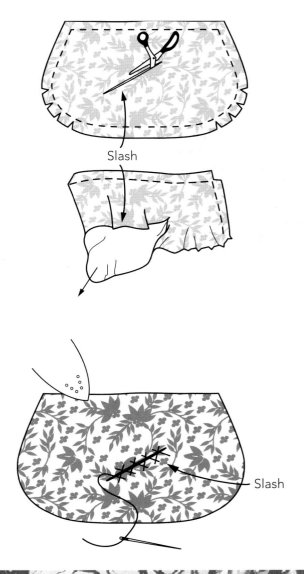

Slash

Slash

5. At this point in the construction, add any other embellishments desired.

6. Once the embellishment is complete, cut a piece of webbed boning for each piece, ½" shorter than the opening edge. Center it along the opening edge, ¼" below the seamline, and whipstitch it into place. The boning provides stability to the upper edge.

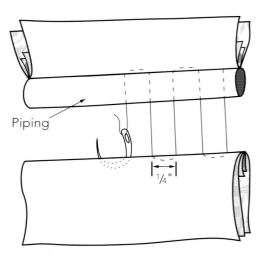

Piping

¼"

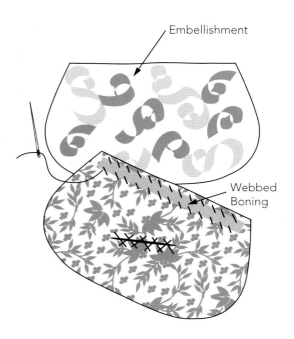

Embellishment

Webbed Boning

7. Pin the pieces wrong sides together and stitch using the curved needle and a running stitch. The object of the game here is to catch the fabrics along the seam and just above the stitching lines. By using a firm but not tight tension, the running stitches will be concealed and the tendency for "dimpling" is reduced.

8. On the lining pieces, press the seam allowances on the opening edges back along the seamlines. Pin right sides together and sew the seam.

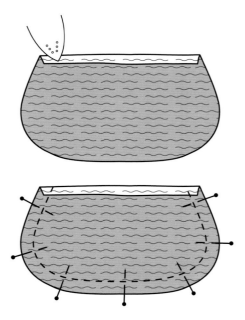

9. Press the seams open for about 1" at the ends of the opening. Miter the corners and press the seam allowances to reduce bulk. Stitch across the seam parallel to the edge to hold the seam allowance open. Fold the lining down along the opening edge seamline and press.

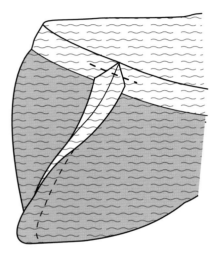

10. Place the lining inside the handbag and, using the curved needle, hand stitch the folded edge of the lining to the base of the piping at the opening edge to finish. The best distance between stitches is approximately ¼", as shown.

HARD BAG CONSTRUCTION

1. Using the handbag pattern piece, cut two pieces of two-ply buckram for the front of the bag and two for the back. Cut one piece on the straight grain and one on the bias for each half for a total of four pieces of buckram. Place one straight-of-grain layer on top of one bias layer and stitch together by machine. Press on one side, turn and press the other side evening out the tension between the two layers. There are no seam allowances added to this pattern piece; the cut pieces will reflect the finished size of the handbag.

> **T I P**
>
> When working with buckram, use your paper scissors for cutting, don't destroy your good fabric scissors! By combining straight-of-grain and bias pieces of buckram, the tendency for the buckram to warp over time is lessened.

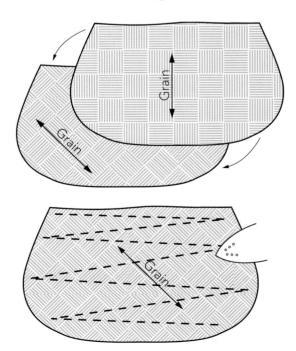

2. Using the pattern piece, cut a piece of "thin cheap" fabric, on the straight grain, for the front and the back. Machine stitch the "thin cheap" fabric to one side of the buckram unit constructed above using a diagonal pattern. This will provide a layer of fabric to stitch to later in the construction process.

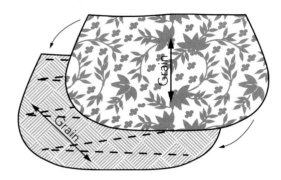

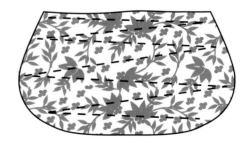

3. Cut a piece of felt interlining, 1" larger around all edges, for each unit of buckram. Machine stitch this felt piece to the buckram unit on the side opposite the "thin cheap" fabric. Clip the curves and press the seam allowances along the sides, not the opening edge, to the thin cheap fabric side of the unit. The seam allowances of the opening edge will be treated later. Topstitch these edges down.

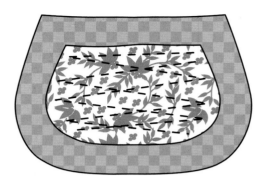

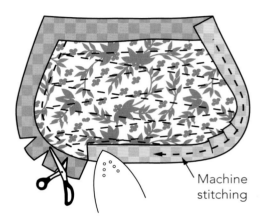

Machine stitching

4. Cut front and back fashion fabric pieces the same size as the felt interlining. Place a piece of fashion fabric, right side out, against the felt interlining on the front and back pieces. Pin in place, making sure the fashion fabric is stretched as tightly as possible.

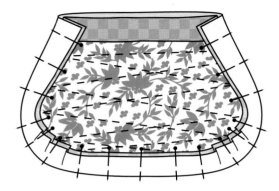

5. Using the curved needle, stitch the fashion fabric to the front and back pieces, making sure the needle catches the "thin cheap" fabric. By just catching the "thin cheap" fabric, the needle is not dulled or broken by passing through the buckram. Stitch the outside edges, but leave the opening edge free, as with the felt interlining.

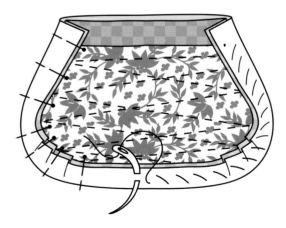

6. The piping is now attached to the outer edge. Before attaching the piping to the outside edge of *one* piece, stitch the piping a second time on the machine with the zipper foot in Position #2 to "snug-up" the bias cover to the fill. The piping will be stitched on by hand

in this step and will not pass through the sewing machine. Piping is added to one piece only, as for the soft bag, since only one piping edge should show when the two halves are sewn together.

7. After attaching the piping to the outer edge of one piece, baste the piping to the seamline of both opening edges. This is easy to do, as the seam allowances were not stitched to the buckram. Simply feel where the edge of the buckram falls, and baste the stitching line of the piping ⅛" outside this edge. Machine stitch with the foot in Position #1.

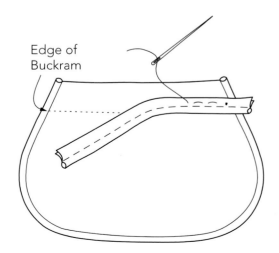

Edge of Buckram

8. Cut two facing strips of lining fabric, 2½" wide and 2" longer than the bag opening. If the bag opening is curved, cut these strips on the bias. With right sides together, place each facing piece along the edge of the bag, and machine stitch on the seamline with the zipper foot in Position #2. Grade the felt to ⅛", and the seam allowances accordingly.

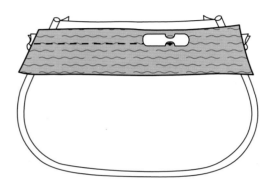

9. Turn the facing strips to the inside next to the "thin cheap" fabric on the front and back pieces, and press. Fold in the ends of the bias strips and press again. Clip to remove any bulk.

10. If additional embellishment is desired, now is the time to do it.

11. With the curved needle, whipstitch the raw edge of the facing strips to the "thin cheap" fabric.

12. Cut front and back lining pieces from the lining fabric and baste piping to the opening edges. Stitch with the foot in Position #2, and then remove the fill from the piping to reduce bulk. Press all seam allowances back.

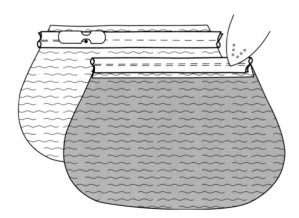

13. With right sides together, pin the lining pieces together and machine stitch along seamlines. Press the seams open at the ends about 1". Miter and press the seam allowances to reduce bulk. Stitch across the seam allowance parallel to the edge to hold in place. Fold down the opening edge on the seamline and press.

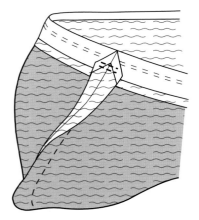

14. The final construction steps of the bag are a bit tricky. Pin the halves together, as you did for the soft bag. Begin hand stitching, 2½"–3" down from the edge, and stitch around the bag to a corresponding point below the edge on the opposite side.

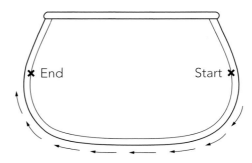

The stitching pattern is illustrated below in an exploded view. Pass the needle through the fold of fashion fabric and felt interlining, at the edge of one of the halves, and then pass through the piping. To take the next stitch, again pass the

needle through the fold of the fashion fabric and felt interlining, at the edge of the other half, and then again through the piping. Stitch length here is ¼". Continue along the entire seam in this manner.

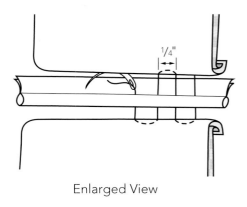

Enlarged View

15. Insert the lining into the bag, positioning the piped edge ¼"–½" above the cut edge of the facing strip. Using the curved needle, stitch across one opening edge through the piping strip. Then stitch the other side. Again, use ¼" stitch length.

16. Finish stitching the sides from the point where the hand stitching started in step 14, stitching up to the opening edge. Knot off at the opening edge. Beading or metal findings will finish off the ends of the opening quite nicely.

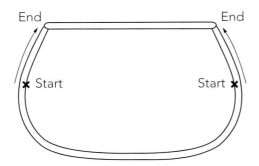

GUSSETS

The hard construction makes a rigid bag that can usually house only a compact and lipstick. You may desire more capacity or more flexibility in your bag. Both of these requirements can be achieved with gussets. Gussets can be used in the soft construction, but they are constructed using typical dressmaker techniques. Here I will outline the technique for adding gussets to the hard construction handbag.

Again, making a model is a good idea, using posterboard or oak tag along with fabric to determine the appropriate shape and capacity for your design. The following construction method is a hybrid of both the hard and soft techniques. I will use a rectangular bag with no flap as the example for the description below, but this method can be adapted to other shapes, with or without flaps.

1.   Begin by cutting the major pieces of the bag from two-ply buckram, on the straight, and on the bias, as in step 1 above. Place one on top of the other and machine stitch these pieces together as described above. Cut pieces of "thin cheap" fabric to cover the buckram units.

Machine stitch to one side of each buckram unit, as in step 2 above.

2.   Place the pieces on felt interlining with the "thin cheap" fabric facing up. Leave ⅛" between the edges of each buckram unit to form the fold in the finished bag. This gap forms what I call the "hinge." Cut the felt out leaving 1" all around for seam allowances.

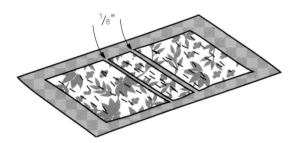

⅛"

T I P

A word about the "hinge"—if a flap is desired on the project or bag, layers of buckram will be prepared for the flap as well. The distance from the "hinged" edge of the flap and the "hinged" edge of the bag is determined by experiment, but 1" is a good starting point.

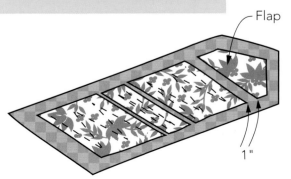

Flap

1"

3. Machine stitch the felt to the three pieces, as in step 3 of "Hard Bag Construction". To make your stitching easier, use fusible web between each buckram unit and the felt to keep all the pieces in line while machine stitching. Press the edges of the felt over the side edges of the buckram unit and topstitch ¼" from the edge. Trim the seam allowances to ¼". The opening edges are left free, as above.

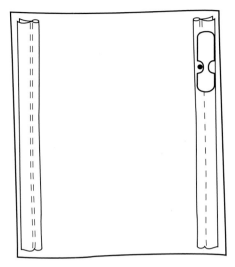

4. Cut the fashion fabric to the same size as the cut felt interlining. Measure the width of the finished bag (actually this will be the length of the rectangle in our discussion). Mark where the seamlines will fall, and baste the piping ¹⁄₁₆" *inside* of this line. This will make the fashion fabric go onto the buckram units tightly.

If a rectangular shape is used, the piping can be machine sewn onto the fashion fabric before the fabric is applied to the buckram unit. If the bag is a complex shape, add the piping by hand, as outlined in step 6 above.

5. Pin the fashion fabric with piping sewn on to the buckram unit, as you did in step 5 above, and hand stitch with the curved needle.

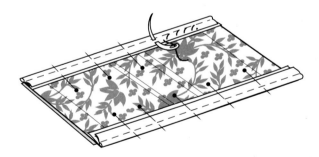

6. Add the piping and facing strips to this assembly, as outlined in steps 6 and 7 above. Once the facing strips are secured, it is time to make the gussets. Measure the depth and width of the bag by folding it into the desired shape. The depth is measured from the edge; the width at the base. The gusset should be ¼" less than the depth of the bag to reduce the bulk at the opening edge of the bag.

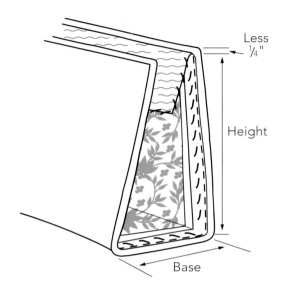

Less ¼"

Height

Base

> **TIP**
>
> I make the gusset pattern after the above work is done, because the variety of thicknesses of fashion fabric will have an impact on how deep the bag will be. The variance can be about ¼"–½". The gusset used here is a rectangle, but any shape can be used, from triangular (with the point of the triangle at the bottom of the bag), to an accordion arrangement. One continuous gusset from one edge across the bottom and up to the other edge is also an option, especially for curved bags. Looking at handbags, both old and new, can give you insight into a variety of shapes.

7.   Draft the seamlines of the gussets onto the back side of the lining fabric, rounding any corners for easier construction. Sew a length of piping across the opening end. Remove the fill from the piping, and stitch this unit to pieces of the fashion fabric, right sides together. If a little more body is desired for the fashion fabric, interline with cotton flannel before sewing.

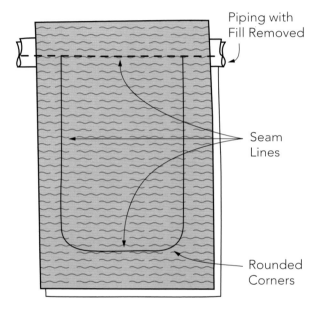

Piping with Fill Removed

Seam Lines

Rounded Corners

8.   After sewing, cut a slash near the bottom, in the lining fabric (see step 3, "Soft Bag Construction"). Turn the work right side out and press. This is the gusset. Use the curved needle again to install the gusset, along with the stitching pattern outlined in step 14 above. Start at the center bottom, and work up along each side to the top. This will ensure the gusset is centered, and will keep the bag from twisting as the result of off-center gussets. As above, use ¼" stitches.

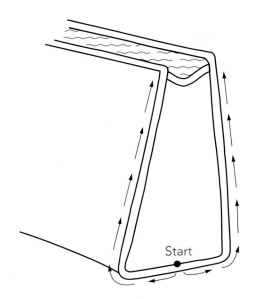

Start

9. To line the gusset bag, draft pieces to reflect the bag and gusset shapes, making the lining 1" shallower than the bag. Finish the gusset opening edges with piping which has the fill removed, as in step 11 above. Hand stitch the lining to the bag with the curved needle.

KENNETH D. KING is known to millions of home sewers as the popular and engaging sewing expert on the Public Television series *Sewing Today*. After graduating from college with a degree in Fashion Merchandising, Kenneth began designing and making fantastic hats that were noted for their unique combination of fantasy and wearability. Soon after, in 1988, he found himself haberdasher to the likes of Elton John, and was soon able to open his own studio in one of the trendiest areas of San Francisco, expanding his creative efforts to include clothing, home furnishings, jewelry, and accessories.

Kenneth's designs are noted for using consummate construction techniques and for being impeccably finished.

His work is shown and collected by museums such as the Los Angeles County Museum of Art and is seen in music videos and on television commercials. Kenneth is also a popular speaker at national sewing conferences both in the United States and Canada, offering sewing tips, comedy, and insights to thousands of home sewers each year.

METRIC EQUIVALENTS

INCHES TO MILLIMETERS AND CENTIMETERS
MM—millimeters   CM—centimeters

Inches	MM	CM	Inches	CM	Inches	CM
⅛	3	0.3	9	22.9	30	76.2
¼	6	0.6	10	25.4	31	78.7
⅜	10	1.0	11	27.9	32	81.3
½	13	1.3	12	30.5	33	83.8
⅝	16	1.6	13	33.0	34	86.4
¾	19	1.9	14	35.6	35	88.9
⅞	22	2.2	15	38.1	36	91.4
1	25	2.5	16	40.6	37	94.0
1¼	32	3.2	17	43.2	38	96.5
1½	38	3.8	18	45.7	39	99.1
1¾	44	4.4	19	48.3	40	101.6
2	51	5.1	20	50.8	41	104.1
2½	64	6.4	21	53.3	42	106.7
3	76	7.6	22	55.9	43	109.2
3½	89	8.9	23	58.4	44	111.8
4	102	10.2	24	61.0	45	114.3
4½	114	11.4	25	63.5	46	116.8
5	127	12.7	26	66.0	47	119.4
6	152	15.2	27	68.6	48	121.9
7	178	17.8	28	71.1	49	124.5
8	203	20.3	29	73.7	50	127.0

METRIC CONVERSION CHART		
Yards	**Inches**	**Meters**
1/8	4.5	0.11
1/4	9	0.23
3/8	13.5	0.34
1/2	18	0.46
5/8	22.5	0.57
3/4	27	0.69
7/8	31.5	0.80
1	36	0.91
1 1/8	40.5	1.03
1 1/4	45	1.14
1 3/8	49.5	1.26
1 1/2	54	1.37
1 5/8	58.5	1.49
1 3/4	63	1.60
1 7/8	67.5	1.71
2	72	1.83

GLOSSARY

Accordion Pleat: A pleat that looks like a zigzag when viewed in cross section.

Back of the Pleat: The fold at the center of the insertion, usually not seen unless it is an accordion pleat.

Bias Cover: The bias strip of fabric that wraps the fill for piping.

Bugle Beads: Tubular beads that are measured by millimeter.

Chainette Fringe: The name of the fringe used when making the tassels. It is rayon, comes in lengths from 2"–30", is available in a wide range of colors, and takes dye easily if color matching is desired. The fringe ends are chainstitched with contrasting thread for shipping and this thread is removed before working.

Crystal Pleat: A very tiny accordion pleat, either purchased or commercially created.

Curved Needles: Allow you to stitch fabrics to flat hard surfaces, as well as inside curves, such as hat linings. No sewing studio should be without them. If they are not available in your area, try the local medical supply—surgical needles are a good substitute. Using curved needles takes a little practice, so don't give up until you master them. You will be rewarded for your diligence!

Depth: The part of the pleat that is concealed when the pleat hangs correctly. It is two times the pleat return.

Fashion Fabric: This is the fabric that will be seen in the finished piece. There are no rules regarding what type of fabric to use or whether the right or wrong side should show in the finished piece (sometimes the wrong side of the fabric is more attractive than the right side).

Fill: The element used to stuff piping. Fills are available in many types, from rattail cord to yarn, and in a variety of sizes.

Flange: Refers either to a strip of twill tape functioning like the seam allowance on piping that is stitched to a decorative cord or trim allowing it to be sewn into a seam; or it is a flat border sewn into a seam that stands out of the seam perpendicular to the surface of the fabric when viewed in cross-section.

Foundation: Rows of chainstitching holding the individual strands of fringe together.

Half-Back: An interfacing piece for the back shoulder area which provides support for the fabric, as well as a place to stitch down the shoulder pads.

Home Row: The first row of beads, usually seed beads, that the mesh cage is built from.

Interfacing: The various materials used to stiffen and support the garment, not to be confused with interlining or underlining. There is usually a separate pattern piece for the interfacing. Interfacing is either sew-in or fusible and, unless otherwise stated, sew-in interfacing is the type discussed in this book.

Knife Pleat: A pleat or series of pleats that lie flat, one over the other.

Knob: The rounded part of the tassel attached to the cord.

Leading Edge: This is the crease on the front side of the pleat. On the outer side is the pleat width, on the under side the pleat depth. It's opposite on the back of the pleat.

Lining: Lining serves two purposes, first, to finish the inside of the piece, and secondly, for aesthetics. It is very satisfying to the sewer to know the inside of the piece is as beautiful as the outside, even when no one else sees the lining.

Mold: Piece of wood or other material that gives shape to the "knob" of the tassel. The fringe of the tassel hangs from the mold, and the mold can be either covered by the fringe or covered by other materials.

Mushroom Pleat: Also referred to as the "Fortuny" pleat, this pleat is created by knife pleating the fabric, and then box pleating over the knife pleats. Fabric can be bought this way or sent out to a commercial pleating establishment to achieve this effect.

Nymo Thread: Spun nylon thread that is as strong as dental floss. This is the "Timex watch" of thread, and you should use Nymo exclusively for bead mesh. It is sized by letter, size B being a good all-purpose size. For best results, iron the thread before use, as ironing will take out the twist and make the thread less prone to knotting.

Opening: Place where the hand enters the pocket.

Pleat Width: The portion of the pleat which extends from the folded edge of the pleat to the fold of the next pleat.

Pocket Bag: The part of the pocket that actually holds the contents of the pocket. In the pockets outlined here, except for the lined patch pocket, the pocket bag is a separate pattern piece.

Pocket Lining: The inside piece of a patch pocket, not to be confused with the pocket bag.

Point: The seed bead in the middle of the bugle-seed-bugle unit. The seed beads actually form a point when they are the uppermost row, and later form an intersection in the mesh.

Prairie Points: Squares of fabric folded into a triangular shape and used as edge trim.

Rattail Cord: Satin cord, about ⅛" thick, usually used for decorative work but often used as fill. This cord is made of rayon and comes in a variety of colors. For the piping techniques in this book, rattail cord will be used unless otherwise stated.

Return: The distance from the fold at the leading edge of the pleat to the back of pleat fold.

Seed Beads: Round-shaped beads available in a variety of sizes.

Shields: These are reinforcing structures attached to the front body interfacing (and sometimes the half-back) that smooth out the dip between the collar-bone and shoulder bone. Shields are not often used in relaxed tailoring.

Shoulder Pad: Also called a shoulder shape, this is inserted into the shoulder at the armhole to support and give shape to the shoulder and sleeve cap.

Skirt: The loose strands of fringe that provide the movement to the tassel.

Sleeve Cap: The upper, curved portion of the sleeve that attaches at the shoulder seam. It is usually eased.

Sleeve Head: A strip of padding inserted into the seam between the sleeve cap and body. It pads out the sleeve cap, eliminating any puckers caused from easing and creates a graceful appearance.

Thinning: Trimming the fill out of the bias cover when the end of the piping is stitched into a seam. This reduces bulk at the ends of piping.

Two-Ply Buckram: Actually two layers fused together—one layer of buckram and one layer of crinoline. The combined layers produce a product that gives good support to the hard handbag.

Underlining or Interlining: These terms refer to fabric that is cut the same size as the fashion fabric and then, with both pieces together, treated as one when sewing for support and weight in the finished piece. These terms are often used interchangeably.

Understructure: A generic term applied to all interfacings, interlinings, and support notions used to create the various effects desired. When your work relies heavily on understructure, it is easy to achieve effects that flatter a figure or even a sofa!

Unit: The bugle-seed-bugle beads sequence that is strung onto the thread. Ultimately these units make up the mesh.

Waist: Found below the knob and above the skirt, the indented section of the tassel that looks like a "waist."

Webbed Boning: Normally used in strapless garments, but it's useful to "stay" the opening edges of the soft bag. The opening edges, which are stitched onto the boning, are then stitched directly onto the inside of the handbag piece without creating a casing.

Welt: The part of a set-in pocket that stands up from the opening seam or seams. It is not a necessary part of a set-in pocket.

Working Above the Fabric: Refers to working only through the holes in the beads to create certain effects. In bead mesh, after the home row is attached to the piece, the needle travels only through the holes in the beads. It doesn't stitch into the tassel at all.

INDEX

NOTES

_____

_____

_____

_____

_____

_____

_____

_____

_____

_____

_____

_____

NOTES